Guardian of the Realm

BOOK THREE OF A TRILOGY
BASED UPON THE LIFE OF
WILLIAM MARSHAL

Richard Woodman

Table of Contents

AUTHOR'S NOTE

Those readers who have followed my evocation of the life of William Marshal in the first two works in this trilogy, *The Knight Banneret*, and *The King's Knight*, will know that in attempting to tell the tale of this remarkable man who survived a period of great instability, it has been necessary to whittle-away much of the complex detail of the times and confine myself to events within the purview of William Marshal himself. I need not repeat the arguments for so doing here.

This third volume brings William Marshal's life to its inevitable conclusion. By 1205, when he went into semi-voluntary exile in Ireland, he was, by the standards of the day, an old man, yet the remaining fourteen years of his life are among the most amazing. From utter disgrace he was recalled by the enigmatic King John and upon John's death he became 'Guardian of the Realm,' effectively Regent of England, during first years of the reign of the boy-King Henry III. John's reign is chiefly known for its 'badness,' his tyranny, his licentiousness, and for his concession to his rebellious Barons at Runnymede, or Runnymead, on the Thames in

1215, which concessions are enshrined in *Magna Carta*, the great charter from which – it is widely supposed – that the liberties of the British people were first established and the power of the monarchy curtailed. This is a gross over-simplification; within days John had repudiated *Magna Carta* to wage a savage winter campaign against his enemies and England was invaded by the French. The defeat of this invasion and the securing of a second *Magna Carta* were, in fact, far more consequential events – and owed more to William Marshal - than that expedient accommodation in the water-meadows of the Thames two years earlier.

Some authorities, eager to make the case for William's nobility of soul, have hinted that he was joint author of the first *Magna Carta*, an assertion that is almost certainly erroneous. However, it is not beyond the possibility that some of his views were enshrined in it, and he was close enough to events to have had some influence in the text, being one of the chief architects of the parley at Runnymead.

William Marshal's more certain - and typically active - part in the subsequent events of 1217 - 1219 was crucial, earning him a place among the statues of Parliamentary heroes in the Palace of Westminster. His reissue of an amended *Magna Carta* in 1216 - the first of several - was an act close to political genius, since it took the wind out of the sails of the rebellious Barons. However, whatever William Marshal's legacy maybe in such a grand arena, he was a man of his age: a professional warrior, both brutal and magnanimous according to circumstances; an opportunist whose sole purpose was to preserve the dynastic line he – the second son of a minor Norman Court functionary (his father had been Marshal of King Stephen's horses) – had established through his marriage to Isabelle de Clare, daughter of Richard Strongbow, Earl of Clare, whose forbears had been Irish Kings. Part of this was the acquisition of land and the complications in terms of fealty that this brought with it in a feudal age are often beyond the easy telling. As Philippe II, known as 'Augustus,' King of France, expanded his own domain at the expense of the House of Anjou whose lords had been both fief-holders of the French King, and Kings of England in their own right, England and France tore themselves apart, to become the 'traditional enemies' that they would remain until within living memory, each vying for a power beyond the grasp of either but which would give to Great Britain that lynch-pin of her foreign-policy – the maintaining of a balance of power in Europe – for the next seven centuries following the defeat of the Dauphin's forces at Lincoln and off Sandwich in 1217.

Lincoln was a battle of great significance, since it marked the beginning of the end of Philippe Augustus's attempts to bring England within his own Pale and William's part in it is as disputed as the actual action itself. Whatever the hypocrisy to the modern mind of a Christian Bishop (in this case Peter Des Roches of Winchester) fighting in armour, the Church liked its own to get the credit, and there seems little doubt that Des Roches played a key role in the victory, but the fact that among the senior commanders of the Royalist force were some extremely experienced professional soldiers, and that William was indisputably commander-in-chief, have led me to take a different view. William's ill-education was common knowledge and, among the lettered, probably made him the butt of jokes and excited the insolence of his peers; snobbery has long been an English vice. Des Roches' own character seems not to have been above criticism and this being the case, I have presumed that at all points William acted as a true leader, suppressing the petty rivalries that were in the genes of these men, took control of the strategy of the brief campaign and the tactical direction of its culmination, using the individual talents of his subordinates to achieve his objective.

As to the battle itself, this is my own recreation, though it seeks to draw on all the (somewhat conflicting) accounts, incorporating all the significant details. Important though

Lincoln was it did not in itself prove decisive. Such were the methods of medieval warfare that, even risking an all-out battle – rather than the tedious taking and exchange of strongpoints – there remained powerful forces under the Dauphin in the south-east. They were ultimately dislodged by a naval battle off Sandwich in Kent, an action that deserves to be better known, and which, it seems to me, awoke the possibilities inherent in English sea-power. Though William was a by-stander in this action, there is ample evidence to suggest that the collision of forces was the outcome of a maritime strategy of his own devising. Historians may argue over the niceties; a novelist has more freedom of assertion. Whatever his short-comings, including his venality, William seems always to have had one eye on something above and beyond the ordinary.

This is, I think, best revealed by what we know of his prolonged death, probably from a carcinoma of the bowel and/or the prostate. The *Histoire*, that biography written shortly after his death, dwells at length upon his last days. Given the well-known vagaries of human memory, and for the purposes of ending a story that did not, of course, terminate with William's death but would lead to further Baronial unrest, I have taken some minor liberties with the detail of those last days at Caversham. From William's perspective as he lay dying, his own sense of duty, alongside his personal agenda, had to be brought to a conclusion from which he might leave this life in a state of grace to meet his God.

Thus, until the moment of his death, the key figure in this period of English History is most certainly William Marshal, Earl of Pembroke, whose dynasty lasted no time at all, but whose legacy – seen in this way, rather than a peerless knight when such a credit was of dubious value – was exceptional, superlative even.

Here, then, is my final 'take' on this remarkable Anglo-Norman knight. Knowing what happened, one cannot ascribe to him any sense of prescience, for he was not only rooted in his time. Unusually, even for his class, he was illiterate, but it seems to me he did possess something of military genius and political vision (feudal though it was), and a strong sense of loyalty to a principle that stretched beyond the concerns of family and personal aggrandisement, though these ran strong within him. It is this, I think, that sets William Marshal apart from his peers and from the general, and generally contemptible, run of politicians in the last seven centuries.
R.W.

PART ONE - JOHN SOFTSWORD 1206 – 1216

CHAPTER ONE - THE LORD OF
LEINSTER 1206 - 1209

William Marshal, Earl of Pembroke and Lord of Leinster, regarded the restless assembly that stood before him in the castle of Kilkenny. Nominally at least they were all vassals of his, the power-brokers of the region who nevertheless owed William their feudal duty. Most, however, wore their obligations lightly, too used to an absentee master in the first place, and, when confronted with a present one, unwilling to surrender the assumed authority by which they had been quietly aggrandising and enriching themselves. Chief among these restives was Meilyr FitzHenry, King John's Chief Justiciar of Ireland, who, having been among the first of the Norman invaders who disturbed the peace of Ireland, regarded William as a new-comer among the Anglo-Norman nobility. Although a great land-owner elsewhere, he was present at the gathering in Kilkenny castle as a tenant of William, holding lands in Leinster and laying claim to other domains within the county, notable Offaly. Moreover Meilyr FitzHenry was related to Henry II by virtue of one of Henry's bastards having impregnated Nest of Deheubarth, a Welsh Princess, with whose family William had gone to war not many months earlier.

William had come into Ireland to escape the frustrations of John's Court and to avoid the King's further displeasure, only to find he had exchanged the Devil's cauldron for the fire beneath it. For almost two years he had played the courtier, aware of John's ill-concealed indifference to an ageing Baron whose usefulness was waning. When John passed over the Channel into Poitou in 1206 on the first of a series of vain expeditions to recover his lost inheritance, he did not summon the Earl of Pembroke; but before going the King settled an outstanding debt to William, leaving William in England in the limbo of uncertainty.

However, on his return, the King blocked William's own long projected departure for Leinster. William recalled that interview, the King vacillating as usual, continuing to refuse to allow William to leave for Leinster, then demanding the surrender of Richard, William's second son, before half-heartedly allowing William to leave the Court with a hint that a passage to Ireland might be possible 'soon'. William and Isabelle's preparations were well-advanced when John rescinded this; William pleaded the necessity of ordering his

– and the King's – affairs in south-east Ireland and ordered his mesnie and household to Milford Haven to embark. Here the King's wrath caught up with William; for his disobedient presumption William had been deprived of the Shrievalty of Gloucester, the Forest of Dean and Ceredigion Castle, all of which greatly reduced his status as a Marcher Lord. In disgust William went aboard his chartered ship.

'I am too old for games,' he grumbled to Isabelle. 'Our boys will be safe enough…'

But if he had thought a quiet life awaited him in Leinster he was mistaken. Despite the iron grip of his old comrade-in-arms and chief bailiff Geoffrey FitzRobert, William had found himself trapped, for the competing claims and internal squabbles of the hard-bitten Norman nobility in Ireland, whose writ derived not merely from conquest over the Celtic chiefs, but from John himself who had once been declared Lord of Ireland by Henry Curtmantle, his father, meant that even in Leinster they claimed a feudal loyalty that entirely by-passed the parvenu William, whose powers were derived entirely through his wife and would return to her upon his death, should he predecease her. And besides the squabbling Anglo-Norman Barony, whatever appearances to the contrary, the Irish chieftains remained unsubdued, while the episcopal power of the Bishops, owing allegiance directly to Rome, was ever a further source of ferment.

Fearful of what hornet's nest William might create, and thanks to the machinations of Meilyr FitzHenry and other Barons close to him, by the end of 1207 he had been summoned home by King John. Along with William John had recalled Meilyr and a host of knights. The feast of Michaelmas approached and with it the chills and rains of autumn. Moreover the gales of the Equinox threatened a quick passage to England, but he was anxious to contact his castellans and constables who held his castles in South Wales and the southern March, and eager to learn of his two sons, William and Richard – now both hostages at John's Court. Most of all he feared further meddling in Ireland when his back was turned and while Meilyr was to accompany him across the sea, Meilyr's influence and intrigues were sufficiently well-known to give little comfort to William by his presence in England. To further weaken William's hand, Geoffrey FitzRobert was ill and it was to the Countess Isabelle that power now devolved.

Thus it was to remind those of his vassals who remained in Leinster of their duty that he had called the present assembly and now he cleared his throat, holding out his right hand which was taken by his wife. Isabelle rose to her feet, obviously pregnant, smiling graciously as William formally presented her as was prescribed by protocol.

'My Lords and gentlemen, many of you will know that His Grace the King has summoned me to attend his presence and in my absence the Lady Isabelle will act in my stead. May I remind you of the duty you owe to her, the grand-daughter of Dermot MacMurrough, King of Leinster. She is your Countess by birth, not in my name, but in that of her father, Richard Strongbow, Earl of Clare, who first enfeoffed you. Since she is heavy with child I charge you to guard her well and in doing so you will do that service to me that is also your meet and bounden duty, both to myself and to the King. For myself, I shall not brook disloyalty, for loyalty I prize above all other chivalric virtues.'

He stared about him as they responded with their declaration of loyalty, a mumbling crowd of men whose faces bore a variety of expressions: of obedience, acquiescence, indifference and, he thought, dissembling. As he withdrew with Isabelle to their private quarters he remarked: 'I did not like what I saw conveyed upon the countenances of many of them, still less could I hear sincerity in their voices.'

To which his wife, ever stoic, replied: 'They will do as they will do, husband. I shall be safe enough. It is my sons for whom I feel the greater fear.'

'John will not harm them...'

'He harmed Arthur of Brittany and is intemperate enough.'

'I think him more circumspect after the loss of his Norman lands.'

'Nevertheless, my Lord, I would have you watch your back. A man of John's stamp is never to be entirely relied upon.'

That evening John D'Earley, the closest of his mesnie and a knight banneret in his own right, came to William.

'My Lord, I am fearful of the outcome of this summons of the King's...'

'You have been talking to the Lady Isabelle...'

'Aye, my Lord,' D'Earley snapped back, his broad and usually untroubled face wearing an expression of extreme anxiety, 'but I can think for myself...'

'So what are you thinking for yourself, John?' asked William, divesting himself of his footwear and bending to fondle the ears of his favourite wolf-hound.

'That my Lord would be wise to take hostages from among those...'

'No, no, no, John,' William waved his friend's advice aside, 'most are to accompany me to England...'

'What about the Chief Justiciar?'

'Him too, though he leaves a following here.' There was a touch of misgiving in William's voice.

'Aye my Lord. He does. And FitzRobert ails. There are those who say he will not live long.' D'Earley's tone was emphatic.

'And you must watch them, John

***

Five weeks later, when November's frosts lay heavy upon the land, William and his large entourage arrived at Woodstock, near Oxford, where the King's Court then lay. John made them welcome with an exaggerated bestowal of largesse that split William's mesnie. To his dismay and public humiliation, and in a process that lasted a few weeks as the Court moved on to Tewkesbury, the King ripped the heart out of William's larger military following, his intimate mesnie and his very family. His nephew, John Marshal, along with Isabelle' brother-in-law, Philip of Prendergast, were both given honours and titles, the younger Marshal being entitled Marshal of Ireland and given a land-grant. They, John declared in a very public snub to William, together with Meilyr FitzHenry, were the chief pillars of his trust in Ireland. Among the other knights and Barons who had supported William against Meilyr and who John now equally conspicuously detached from Earl William, were the Marcher lords William of Barry, David and Eustace de la Roche, Gilbert d'Angle, Robert FitzMartin de Cemaes, Robert

FitzRichard de Haverford and Adam de Hereford. Although almost impossible to refuse, acceptance of the King's grants and gifts amounted to a wholesale defection of all those who had accompanied William from Kilkenny.

It was brought gleefully to William's ears that one of his courtiers asked the King why he had not offered John D'Earley some inducement to abandon the ageing paladin, only to be told that he, the King, had no wish to find himself infected of a mange that only too closely clung to an old hound's skin. In fact William had left a reluctant D'Earley in Ireland in support of the Lady Isabelle, charged with the defence of half of Leinster, but there could be no doubt of John's disregard for William, exposing him politically and militarily, leaving him to recall Isabelle's – and D'Earley's - warnings.

Faced with this impasse William affected a supreme indifference, maintaining a cool courtesy towards all that at first was seen as folly, as a too-easily given acquiescence to John's whim, but – as John's volatile character played out in vacillating policies – many came to appreciate William's quiet dignity and restraint as a mark of great courtesy.

To his private consternation William also received word from his wife that Meilyr FitzHenry's adherents had risen in revolt almost the moment the sails of William's ships had vanished over the horizon. Meilyr's troops had carried out a series of *chevauchées*, raiding William's lands and taking the port and borough of New Ross where William had been busy establishing a presence. Hearing of his men's successes Meilyr, in presenting them to the King, suggested William's officers, chief among them John D'Earley, be recalled to England, a plan to which the King acceded. He also granted the Chief Justiciar permission to return himself to Ireland with a free hand to secure the whole of Leinster in the King's name, cutting William out of the political picture and disinheriting the Lady Isabelle

Not knowing that William already knew of the action taken by Meilyr's men, the Chief Justiciar came armed into William's presence to inform him of the turn events had taken.

'My Lord Marshal,' FitzHenry began smoothly, regarding William with some contempt as he sat dictating to his personal clerk, Thomas, 'I am directed by the King's Grace to inform you…'

Waving Thomas and his papers away, William did not trouble himself to rise, but took a wrinkled apple from a bowl of fruit set before him and bit into it with a crunch that interrupted the triumphant Meilyr.

'That you have broken your promise of loyalty, taken my land and the borough of New Town, and have had the insolence to carry out raids and make war upon a peaceful land.' William said, munching his way noisily through the pippin, unfazed by Meilyr's malevolent bombast, then tossed aside the core for his hounds to fight over and looked up at his enemy.

'You are a false fellow, FitzHenry, and your society displeases me. As you are about to leave for Ireland, I would take it as a kindness, if such a thing exists with you, to absent yourself from my company without delay.'

For a moment Meilyr stood non-plussed, then he retorted, 'I have heard the Lady Isabelle's heart may be laid siege to, having only a cur to defend it.'

'Get out,' William said quietly, 'get out before I strike you dead.'

It was a bold remark to make to a man fully armed. William's sword lay upon a side table and had he made a move to seize it, FitzHenry could most certainly have cut William down. But William made no move to rise and simply sat confronting his declared enemy, a look of utter contempt upon his face. Meilyr FitzHenry had no option but to retreat, for the dishonour of attacking a seated, unarmed man would redound to his ultimate discredit and so he forbore the temptation.

William gave FitzHenry a few moments to clear his chambers and then sent for Thomas. 'That despatch I was dictating, bring it hither that I may make my sign manual upon it.'

Thomas hung his head. 'My Lord, knowing its gravity, I sent it at once, before the Chief Justiciar closed the gates. Forgive me…'

William smiled his satisfaction. 'There is nothing to forgive, Thomas, you did right by me and I thank you for it. Come, pour some wine. By-the-by, who took it?'

'Edgar, my Lord.'

William frowned, his mood changing. 'He that is but lately come into my service?' It seemed to William that Thomas's initiative, welcome though it was, might have been placed in entirely the wrong hands. He recalled the man as not having been much in evidence, a man of Saxon blood, if William was not mistaken, well enough looking, to be sure, with a frank and open appearance, but with a withered arm. A man with something of the cloister about him, and not enough of the physique for a confidential go-between.

'Forgive me my Lord,' Thomas said again, 'but he is known to me, my eldest sister's eldest son. Knowing he could read and write, I brought him hence to find a place for him. But for his mis-shapenness he would be fitted for one of your guards, my Lord, for he is both a good swordsman and excellent

24

horseman and therefore fitted for such a task as I have laid upon him.'

'He fights with his left hand?'

'Aye, my Lord, and writes with it too, and in a good, clear script.'

William regarded his clerk with a shrewd eye. 'You quietly taught him his penmanship and ability with letters did you not?'

Thomas flushed and looked down.

'With a view to insinuating him into my household...'

'My Lord!' Thomas protested, looking-up, but William was smiling at him. 'Come where is that wine? If the fellow proves as you commend him, we shall make good use of him, I have no doubt.'

***

But that was the last happy thought William had that long winter. Meilyr and his entourage crossed over into Leinster shortly in early January, after Epiphany, and by the middle of the month a series of furious gales cut off all communication with Ireland. William was obliged to trail in the King's wake, neither seeking John's approbation, nor acting with anything other than a strict propriety. He sent and received messages to and from his remaining castellans, bailiffs and constables, those whom John had left him in a slow reduction of the Earl's powers and he also made peace with his nephew, John Marshal, who approached his uncle in secret, eager for a private understanding, but the accommodation – welcome though it was – brought no real consolation: what a man could do once, he could do again.

In many ways the increasingly open hostility of the King made it easier for William to remain aloof. It betrayed John's fear of him, yet William knew it goaded the King; on the other hand it offered him no pretext for directly attacking William. Instead John confiscated the Leinster lands of John D'Earley, whom John knew was as close to William as any son, informing William by letter that his orders recalling D'Earley to England, sent by way of FitzHenry, had been ignored, an intolerable situation for the King. But William held his counsel close and refused to react. Not the least of his reasons was to forbear from giving the King the slightest pretext to take back more of his own and his vassals' lands than he had already done.

The King's arbitrary and inconstant character could not cope with a stony wall of polite indifference. Being a man of violent intemperance, William's cool acceptance of the *status quo* riled him. Whilst William offered John every sign of obedience and deference, a display of a *politesse* that, while observers quailed at the outcome, earned William greater and greater respect for his courtliness, it inflamed the King to that petty, petulant impotence for which he was so well-known.

Matters came to something of a head at Guildford, at the end of January, when John came across William walking quietly with his clerk. William, seeing the King, stopped to make his obeisance. Instead of passing by, John walked up to William and, without greeting, asked in an insinuating tone of voice William knew well: 'My Lord Marshal, hast heard the news from Leinster?'

'No Your Grace, I have heard nothing.'

'I am better informed then,' John sneered, 'Kilkenny is under siege, the castle closely invested. Your household knights, in an attempt to relieve the Lady Isabelle within it, have been ambushed and cut to pieces. John D'Earley was mortally wounded and is now dead and the Lady Isabelle must shortly come to her senses and surrender the castle of Kilkenny...'

John peered up at William's immobile features, expectantly awaiting a reaction he might have rehearsed when at stool or in some other private place of meditation, but William, confident that no such news had crossed from Ireland, stared back at the King. His face flushing with a growing anger, John prodded William.

'Well, what think you of this intelligence?'

William shook his head gravely.

'My Lord King, the death of D'Earley and his companions is indeed tragic for both of us, for they were your knights as much as they were mine, as obedient to me as I have been to you these last months. If Kilkenny is under siege it is being held against rebels to your Crown and my Lady's authority under it.'

John opened his mouth to retort then snapped it shut and turned away, muttering. William bowed as the train of courtiers followed their master.

'God's blood, the man tries my patience,' William murmured to himself and catching the eye of the faithful Thomas. 'Did you hear what the King said, Thomas?'

'Aye, my Lord. We would assuredly have heard something if there was substance to it,' Thomas said, reassuringly. William nodded.

***

When, on Ash Wednesday, late that February, the weather abated sufficiently for news to finally reach the Court, William's old heart beat with a quiet satisfaction. Unable quite to believe the first rumoured tittle-tattle, he had Thomas send word to his nephew Edgar, now fully acknowledged as William's confidential messenger, who, under the pretext of carrying letters of administration into the Earl's

Pembrokeshire domain, rode for the little port of Solva to determine the truth. Edgar executed his commission well, returning with the full story before it was common knowledge at Court, though the King had known it for some days, deliberately concealing it.

Ushered into William's presence, Edgar, still in his travelling clothes, his cloak spattered by the rains of late winter, rubbing his withered arm and aching from hours in the saddle, bowed to William. Despite his woebegone appearance, however, it was clear to William and the ever attentive Thomas that Edgar's tidings were good, for the man's eyes gleamed.

'What news man? Come, a glass of wine...'

'I thank thee, my Lord, but later,' replied the under-clerk his voice imbued with excitement. 'My Lord, the Lady Isabelle has Meilyr FitzHenry a prisoner in her keeping in Kilkenny, the promise of his son as a hostage and the promises of others disloyal to your Lordship to surrender their sons hostage to the Countess. Philip de Prendergast and...'

'That is good news indeed,' William broke in, 'But what of John D'Earley? Tell me of him?'

'He is safe, my Lord...'

'Thanks be to God,' interjected William piously crossing himself. 'He and my Lady have been much in my thoughts and more in my prayers of late.'

'Would my Lord hear more?'

'Aye, if you have more to tell.'

'Oh aye, my Lord, for it seems that matters passed thus: My Lord FitzHenry and his force, having been delayed by contrary weather, arrived late in Ireland with the King's order to Messire D'Earley and his close companions to return to England. As you well know, my Lord Marshal, since my Lord FitzHenry came hither with my Lord at the fall of the leaf last, FitzHenry's following rose and made war against the forces my Lord left in Leinster, enjoying some success. However, during the winter months, D'Earley and others, including Lord de Lacy, taking counsel of the Lady Isabelle, contended with the rebels for control of the country.

'When, therefore Meilyr FitzHenry landed he had one of his mesnie convey to John D'Earley, my Lord de Lacy and the other Barons charged with the defence of Leinster, their recall from the King, D'Earley rejected the letters.'

'Ho!' Exclaimed William, his attention fixed upon the under-clerk's animated face. Thomas had chosen well. The man impressed him, as did so many who could read and write with fluency, for they seemed capable of grasping and ordering facts in a way which often astonished William for whom they formed nothing but patterns in his brain. He could 'read' the country and often divine the intentions of his enemies in the field with an impressive prescience; he could devise strategies, order a line of march and organise military stores, reinforcements, remounts, even fire-wood and watering places; he could contrive an advantageous order of battle, even sniff out a plot at Court and see dissembling in a man's eyes, but the precise marshalling of facts in such a close and ordered narrative by means of the *aides memoire* that he knew Thomas maintained, was a skill of the literate which he both admired and envied.

'Is there more, Master Edgar?' he enquired with an almost boyish eagerness now that his anxieties regarding Isabelle and D'Earley were laid to rest.

'Aye, my Lord.'

'Then tell it, tell it.'

'It is reported that on receiving FitzHenry's emissary, Thomas Bloet...'

'Brother to Ralph Bloet of my mesnie and half-brother to FitzHenry himself through Nest ap Iorwerth ap Owain of Deheubarth?'

'The same, my Lord.'

'God's wounds, what a tangle, but pray go on.'

31

"Sir," D'Earley said to Bloet, "Contrary to your expectations, the land does not lie at your feet. We have several knights of your master's household held prisoner awaiting ransom and his garrisons under siege."

"You will lose your lands in England if you defy the King," Bloet apparently interposed, to which John D'Earley responded:

"Better to lose land of our own than to lose our Lord's land to whose defence we have sworn and by the doing of which we shall lose honour and the love of our Lord of Pembroke. Besides," D'Earley, had then added, apparently dissembling, "I see more of FitzHenry's hand in this than that of the King who did ever love my Lord the Marshal for his steadfastness…"

"This is the King's seal," Meilyr's man had expostulated, showing the charge upon which he met them.

"Perhaps it is,' D'Earley is said to have responded, peering at it, "I would not know, by my troth, but my Lady, the Countess Isabelle, has charged us to hold these lands in the name of our Lord, and I am bound by my oaths to My Lady and my Lord, to uphold their legitimate rights until my Lord, who resides at the King's Court and owes His Grace allegiance, orders me otherwise."

'Having turned FitzHenry's man Bloet away, D'Earley awaited the reaction, ordering up his forces to cover the landing place whereupon, two hours later Philip de Prendergast arrived and, seeing which way the wind blew, let it be known that he would come to terms. The following day others among the chief knights of Leinster, for fear of losing their lands, and knowing the King's hold on them was weaker than their own, made their composition with the Lady Isabelle, some with a son, others bereft of offspring with their younger brothers. ''Tis said Kilkenny castle and the Lacy's strongholds harbour more rebels than loyalists,' Edgar quipped as he brought his narrative to its conclusion.

'Well,' remarked William himself pouring wine for the under-clerk and a second pot for Thomas, 'I am indebted to you, Master Edgar, for my mind was much troubled on these matters. I shall sleep the easier tonight knowing that the Lady Isabelle and John D'Earley are safe, though I do conjure you both, as you love me, to show no sign of this triumph, even after the King hears of it.'

King John heard of it a week later, summoning William from Chepstow to Bristol, and asking him whether he had heard anything from Ireland. William dissembled, replying that he had heard nothing from the Lady Isabelle, which of itself was true, telling the King, 'Sire, when I departed from

33

Ireland I knew of no man who intended war against me and mine, nor against the King's Grace.'

John stared at William, whose bland expression gave nothing away, then smiled. Happily Isabelle's dispatch caught up with him two days later, by which time the King had shrugged off the mishap as of no consequence. William's reference to the King's Grace implied all had been attempted by rebels, that as far as he was concerned Meilyr FitzHenry had acted falsely and against the natural order of things, giving John sufficient pretext to resolve the matter by a formal ceremony of demanding Leinster from William and then reconferring it upon him. This *demarché* reduced William's powers a little, allowing the King a small sense of victory, but Meilyr FitzHenry was deprived of Offaly which was returned to William.

FitzHenry's fall from grace was permanent; he was deprived of his office as Chief Justiciar and retired to his estates but William was exhausted by these troubles. He sought the King's permission to retire to Leinster.

'My Lord King, I would go thither and keep thy peace. I am old and of little use to Your Grace and would fain settle Leinster and see order in that rich and promising land.'

John tugged at his beard, regarding William through narrowed eyes, then he thrust out his right hand with its regal ring. William bent and kissed it.

'Go,' John said dismissively, 'and may God or the Devil go with you. We shall have no further use for you in our Kingdom of England for your bones are old and deserving of rest.'

William drew back, made his obeisance, turned on his heel and was gone.

***

With his Countess beside him, William sat in his chair of state in the hall of Kilkenny castle and regarded the two men before him. Arraigned behind William were a number of his chief Barons and knights, among them John D'Earley, his broad, open features split by his famous grin as he too stared at Meilyr FitzHenry and his heir. Their heads bowed in every outward appearance of solemn contrition, father and son awaited William's expression of displeasure.

'Is there any person present that wishes to speak for this man?' William asked formally, whereupon Countess Isabelle stirred beside him.

'My Lord, he is false and besides the King, betrayed both you and me…'

'I did not betray His Grace the King,' FitzHenry broke in, his head coning up, his eyes ablaze with protest.

'Say you that you were in connivance with His Grace?' Isabelle interjected sharply before William could respond.

Perceiving he had been entrapped, FitzHenry cast about vainly for support; there was none, for while everyone present knew the untrustworthy King played a double game, what always mattered in such circumstances was the moment, and at that moment he, Meilyr FitzHenry was a lamb surrounded by wolves. Having opened his mouth in vain, FitzHenry clamped it shut again.

My Lord FitzHenry,' William said in a mild and judicial tone, 'the best that can be said of your conduct is that you have been misled. I should not be here had I not come with the King's full confidence and his royal blessing. You were here at Michaelmas last and swore your allegiance to my Lady in my absence and, even though you accompanied me into England, you had laid a plot and rebellion against her and for that I must hold you responsible. You shall leave your son in our custody against you continuing good behaviour and retire to your lands, as for breaking your word I have here,' William broke off and motioned to Thomas who rose from the table at which he recorded the council's meeting and stepped forward holding a parchment, 'an instrument surrendering to me as of this moment, your fortress at Dunamase, and thereafter...' William let FitzHenry peruse the conditions of his release.

Meilyr's took the document from Thomas and scanned it, his face draining of all colour and his hand shaking as he read it to the end. When he had finished he looked up at William.

'My Lord Marshal,' he protested, his voice cracking, 'this cannot be... *All* my lands to you upon my death? My son an alleged bastard? This is infamous...'

'No, FitzHenry,' William's voice was now hard, 'this is rough justice, for you requited my love with rebellion, planned and carried out behind my back, while you pretended amity in my company. You may thank me for my leniency and that I do not take your lands within your own lifetime. As for the alleged bastardy of your son here, it is commonly spoken of and, if it is infamous, I can only say that many hold it to be true. It may be that you disregard him. Let me see to his future; you have my word I shall treat him as if he were my own for I know what it is to be held a hostage against a father's good conduct. Now, do you go in peace, for know you this, the King my master has confirmed my Lordship of Leinster. If you live quietly I shall not trouble you beyond your feudal duty to supply me in men-at-arms, but if you seek alliance with any other Lord or Chief in Ireland, Wales or England, I shall utterly destroy you. Now, your oath upon this, your sign upon this document and the hand of your son.'

'That was well done husband,' Isabelle remarked after FitzHenry had withdrawn and left his ten year old boy, in William's custody.

'I cannot stand bad faith, Belle,' he replied, calling for wine.

'I would that you had treated all that followed him in like manner,' she added, 'for I trust none of them.'

'Well, we shall see…'

'This is not a quiet place, William. Would that it was, but no-man can settle here without offending his neighbour and conquest is not enough, one must hold what one has with an iron hand.'

CHAPTER TWO - THE INCONSTANT KING 1209 - 1214

Isabelle's words were no warning; they took on the character of a prophecy. As William sought to ground his administration into the feudal order of his lands in England and the Welsh March, he found himself in arms against an uprising of the indigenous Irish led by Ailbe Ómáelmuaid, the Cistercian Bishop of Fearns and a former associate of King John from the days when John had been Count of Mortmain. Such was the ferocity of William's campaigning and his prejudice against the Bishop, that Ailbe successfully sought a ban of excommunication against William, an Interdict that would follow William for the rest of his life. William felt the excommunication keenly, but his preoccupations were temporal, rather than spiritual, for by now he had little sympathy with anything he saw as disloyalty or disruption of what he conceived to be the King's peace, believing that as Lord of Leinster under John's hand, he was bound to supress all disorder.

In part this uncompromising response was engendered by the fact that his two eldest sons were in the King's hands, but he was also tired of war and so, when compelled to wage it, did so with a savagery intended to bring it the quicker to a termination. He could, he felt, make his peace with the church later.

But such a neat, self-serving policy received a strong check late in 1209 when in spite of the winter gales a fellow Marcher Lord, William de Briouze, washed-up upon the Wicklow strand with his household and most of his mesnie. De Briouze had married into the family of Hugh de Lacy, Lord of Ulster, whose support of Isabelle during the rebellion of FitzHenry's making, William appreciated. Thus he and Isabelle welcomed De Briouze and his entourage to Kilkenny. It was only after this gesture that William learned that De Briouze had foolishly and precipitately risen against the King and that he harboured a rebel in his own stronghold.

The news infuriated William and he privately raged in his chamber, Isabelle white-faced before him as he paced up and down in a frenzy.

'I am most assuredly compromised!'

'My Lord, still you ire, 'twill do you no good, you will bring on an apoplexy!'

'God forgive me but an apoplexy would do me more honour than this impasse. I must, of necessity pitch De Briouze out and send him north to his kinsmen in Carrickfergus…'

'Have you intelligence of the King's intentions?' his wife asked.

'Do I need it?' William stopped his pacing and ran his right hand through his mane of grey hair. 'By all the Saints, John will be here when the season opens…'

'And you must join him. Better still, William, that you pass over to Pembroke and receive him there if he is coming into Ireland.'

William nodded, calming himself. 'You speak with wisdom, Belle, but oh what a fool De Briouze is…can he have fallen so far in the King's favour that he must make war against his Liege Lord?'

'Not all men are like you, husband,' Isabelle remarked drily.

'Huh,' William grunted. He walked to the narrow lancet in the keep and stared out, seeing nothing, his mind seething. Then he turned back into the chamber. 'I must send Edgar to warn me of the King's coming…'

***

William bent his knee before John at Pembroke Castle in June 1210. He had come hither with a handful of his mesnie to welcome the King and assure him of his loyalty.

'But you harboured a rebel, My Lord of Pembroke,' John said, tugging his beard in secret delight that he had the upper hand.

'Unknowingly, my Lord King.'

'Unknowingly? Come, come, does a man turn-up in midwinter with his whole household and convince a man of your intelligence that he is taking a hunting trip into Ireland without you suspecting some other reason?'

'Your Grace, the King's cause, upheld by the Countess Isabelle in my absence, had some obligations to my Lord De Lacy of Ulster. It was for this reason that William De Briouze was offered hospitality. When I knew the reason for his leaving of England I ordered him to leave and am here to protect my loyalty.'

'Words, words, words; you were ever good with words, Marshal,' John snarled, using that most junior of all William's titles, calling for wine and waving William out of his presence.

William was furious but could see no purpose in protesting. He knew John's temper and the Angevin character. Besides, he was in no mood for further prolonged conflict and wanted only to return quietly to Isabelle's side.

William accompanied John's army back to Waterford where it landed, the largest Anglo-Norman force ever seen in Ireland.

John marched on Kilkenny and quartered this vast assembly of eight hundred and ten knights and men-at-arms with over one thousand foot-soldiers upon William until he was ready to march north. Before he departed he summoned William and, his face a mask of vindictiveness, took from him the keys of Dunamase Castle.

'You obtained the place with ease,' the King remarked, 'and lose it likewise.'

***

John's campaign in Ireland was among the few military successes of his troubled reign, though it was not without set-backs and left a legacy of hatred. He took Carrickfergus and scattered De Briouze and his Lacy allies before marching on Dublin where, in the full flush of victory, he again accused William of disloyalty. Now, however, William was indignant; he had supported the King's arms in his Irish foray and had given no cause for John to suspect him. It was, as Isabelle had pointed out but a few weeks earlier, as if William's great age and experience, his long service to the House of Anjou, and his steadfastness, acted like an itch to a man of John's inconstancy.

'You are a reproach to him, husband, and while he knows he would be a fool to destroy you, he needs must keep you at a distance for fear he relies upon you too much and thereby displays his own weakness.'

'That is cold consolation,' William responded, slipping into bed next to her. 'He has summoned me to Dublin.'

'Render to him that service that he requires,' Isabelle advised. William nodded.

But the King's new charge of bad faith irked him when he was confronted with it in front of the assembled Barons. He bit his tongue, even as the King demanded as a hostage the person of 'he whom you love like a son, that mangy cur John D'Earley'.

William was about to protest the injustice of the King's extortion, but he recalled Isabelle's words and some sixth sense warned him that this was not the moment to cross John. Instead he drew himself up and bowed to the King.

'As God is my witness, Your Grace, I challenge any man to contest my guilt of this charge in armed combat.' He had thrown down the gauntlet in such a way before and, once again, the response was the same. No-one moved to uphold John's honour, a fact not lost on the King who glowered at his Barons and called for more wine.

Nevertheless, William was obliged to acquiesce. The best he could do was to ensure D'Earley knew that he would seek to make his friend's incarceration as bearable as possible as John was sent a prisoner to Nottingham.

But while King John returned to England and William withdrew to Kilkenny, the King left his new Justiciar, John de Gray, the Bishop of Norwich, to harry the Irish chieftains out of little more than pure malice. When the Irish King of Connacht refused to give up hostages to John, De Gray led a mighty and brutal *chevauchée* into Connacht's lands, only to provoke an equally fearsome uprising led by Cormac O'Melachlin. O'Melachlin twice defeated the Bishop in open battle and went on a bloody rampage of his own at the end of which several Anglo-Norman fortresses lay in smoking ruins.

William took no part in these unhappy affairs, though the tide of disruption and displacement affected Kilkenny. He had lost his chief confidant in England with the death of Hubert FitzWalter, the Archbishop of Canterbury, and despite his private desire to rusticate in his Irish lands, he had hoped to do so in some semblance of tranquillity. The confiscation of most of William's Welsh privileges and possessions by a suspicious King John, the hostage taking of John D'Earley and the continued holding of his two sons, William and Richard, gnawed at William and brewed discord between man and wife. Though Isabelle's concerns for her boys was, as William constantly assured her, needless, he had had word

45

that the King had ordered John D'Earley kept in close confinement in Nottingham Castle, deprived of those easements usual in such cases as his was. William knew that the King wished William to know of this, such casual cruelty being a direct threat to William and a mark of the King's continuing displeasure.

Watching events in England as best he might from the remote fastness of Kilkenny, William had Thomas send Edgar abroad to gather intelligence on the pretext of visiting those castellans still in the Earl's service. He was less troubled by the news that John de Gray had suffered further defeats, though of the spiritual world. Having been nominated by John Archbishop-elect of Canterbury, De Gray had been set aside by Papal Interdict. John's refusal to accept the Pope's decision that Cardinal Stephen Langton should become John's new Prelate had aroused the righteous wrath of Pope Innocent III.

But neither the excommunication of all England nor his own personal spiritual isolation troubled William. Baptism of infants continued, as did the offices ministering to the penance of the dying, while the Cistercians were chief among a number of religious Houses claiming exemption from Innocent's proscriptions.

Aware that affairs in England were going ill for John, William canvassed opinion among his chief Barons and dictated a letter of support to the King, offering him men and horses, even his own lance. John responded, ordering William to stay where he was, to support De Gray and hold Ireland above all things. However, he was to send the King money, the better to equip his two sons for war in the King's service.

However, when he heard news of a serious uprising against John among the Barons of the north of England, news which told of a great plot to turn the whole Kingdom against the King, William stirred. At first he did not believe such an extravagant tale, for some spoke of the murder of the King, others of his being sold to the Welsh, but affairs took a more serious turn when news arrived at Waterford that the French King, Philippe Augustus, provoked by John's repeated sallies into Poitou, and well aware of John's weakness at home, was preparing a great fleet, and embarking troops for invasion.

This was too much for the old man. Against Isabelle's advice, he sent out a summons and obtained the pledges of almost the entire Anglo-Norman Barony of Ireland in support of the King and on 15 August 1213 he joined King John near Dover. William arrived at the head of five hundred knights and their mesnies, making their last day's riding armed and accoutred for war. William, under his banner of a red lion rampant on a ground of green and gold, his surtout bearing the same device over a coat of mail and his helm upon his saddle-bow, led the column, glittering in the sunshine, into John's encampment outside a Templar House near Dover.

If, with this addition of power to John's army mustering to oppose the French, he expected a warm welcome, William was to be disappointed. John's initial greeting was cold and formal and William had been in his company for two days before he was summoned to the King's Council. He had wisely not pressed his presence upon the King, but spent his time seeing to the ordering of his large following. When the summons came, William, dressed in mail and surtout, entered the King's chamber with one of his close household knights, William Waleran and his clerk Thomas at his side. John's appearance shook William; the younger man had grown bloated with easy living and indulgence. He sat, as William long remembered him, slumped in his chair at the head of an otherwise unoccupied table with a goblet of Bordeaux wine before him. Behind him were ranged those Barons still loyal to him, among them William's own sons and his old friends Geoffery FitzPeter and William Longsword, Earl of Salisbury.

Left hand on sword hilt, William made his obeisance and John stared at him for some moments. William stood and bore the scrutiny, he had been in the service of the House of Anjou for too long to expect anything remotely like a courteous respect for his grey hairs, while his welcome, or lack of it, had given him nothing to hope for but further exhausting service. But for once John surprised him.

Ordering the chamber cleared, John waited until the two were alone.

'My Lord William,' he said intimately, his expression suddenly somehow fallen, exhausted, grown desperate, a sensation confirmed by what followed. 'Tell me upon your oath that you had no part in the conspiracy among my northern Barons.'

William was genuinely shocked at the accusation. Was this eternal suspicion how John saw him? No wonder John D'Earley suffered in Nottingham.

'Upon my oath, my Liege,' he responded with sharp, even indignant, formality, dropping to one knee. 'Did I not offer my power to Your Grace and am I not here with the chivalry of Ireland at my back.'

John expelled his breath; it was none too sweet. He motioned William to rise and draw a camp stool forward so that he might take a seat at board. 'Draw close. You will rejoin my Council,' he said, his voice low, confidential, 'and I shall release John D'Earley, and place your son William in his charge. Your boy Richard I shall place with Thomas de Sandford. Besides the displeasure of that gang of traitors I have nursed in my bosom here in England, Philippe of France has Papal blessing to seize my throne if I do not submit and accept that dog Langton in the See of Canterbury. The Papal Legate Pandolpho is here to press upon me submission to Papal authority…'

John was clenching the stem of his goblet and almost grinding his teeth as he confided in William.

'Christ's bones,' he went on, 'I would fain pass over again into Poitou to strike at the bastard's under-belly, but he has troops in Flanders and a great fleet assembled there to carry them hither. The Dauphin Louis will rule England under his father, once I am deposed and,' and here John beat the table with his other fist, clenched like a hammer-head, 'my northern Barons, God rot them, refuse service and simmer and plot against me.'

The intensity of John's feelings was plain; sweat now poured off his brow and William observed an Angevin Prince uncharacteristically mastering his prodigious rage. The King suddenly let go of the goblet, leaned forward and dug his fingers into William's shoulder, gripping him with a ferocity that betokened a fear of losing William. William dropped his eyes.

'Look at me,' John hissed and William felt the spittle and the stink of John's breath upon his face. He looked at the King.

'Thou wast ever faithful to my House, William Marshal, and owe all that you have to my father and my brothers…' John's appeal, clear though it was in implication, petered out and William was quick to fill the void, so that there could be no doubt, for he was thinking fast.

'My Liege,' he said, braving the King's breath, 'you can have no cause to doubt me, ill-used though I have been at time if it is that that gives you anxiety.'

'Your lands in Normandy give me anxiety.'

The King's grip on William's shoulder grew fiercer. William's Norman estates were held enfeoffed under Philippe Augustus and the question of divided loyalty had caused a schism with the King of England before, but William saw now a slender hope of securing a greater legacy than those first acquisitions. John had made him an Earl, a great Marcher Lord, even though he had also stripped him of much of his Welsh lands after his falling-out with the King. Greatly desirous as he was of recovering his fiefdoms in south Wales, to ask directly for them at such a moment would not mollify John in such a mood but William knew the chalice John offered him held both gall and wine, if not outright poison. Yet he must not lose the initiative this moment gave him.

Before responding directly to the King he asked in a low voice to match the King's:

'Before you go over into Poitou, Your Grace, what measures can we put in train to oppose the present threat of the French invasion?'

Perceiving that he had won his man, John relaxed his grip and answered. 'I have called a Council for this afternoon. William de Salisbury has a fleet ready to sail against them, they lie in The Downs awaiting the order to sail against the French ships at Damme.'

'Then give it, Your Grace, without delay, without the Council, if needs be and,' he paused, 'if I may speak freely?' John inclined his head. 'Submit to Pope Innocent; half of Philippe's justification for war will be removed at a stroke and the people of England will rejoice. You have the Legate here…'

'Innocent will demand an indemnity.'

'Pay it, Sire. Submit England to the Pope, obtain his protection, Philippe will be out-manoeuvred, send an embassy to the Emperor, for I hear there is little love lost between Otto and Philippe, the King of France being engrossed to the Empire's detriment…'

John nodded. He seemed both to deflate from the tension of the moment and drew fresh breath for the future.

'Aye, aye, your counsel is wise…' A flicker of possibility was lit in John's eyes and he drew himself up in his chair, but William had not finished with him yet.

'As for the allegiance I owe Philippe of France for my lands in Normandy, My Liege,' he pressed on, knowing he had the King's ear as he had not had it for years, 'I am made Earl of Pembroke and Leinster by your gracious hand…' William deliberately let the sentence hang.

'Go on,' John prompted.

'What more can I say than that I was ever ready to render you and your House that service to which I was bound. What lay in your power before lays in your power today; in Normandy lies my past, in your Kingdom lies my future.'

The two men regarded each other for some moments then John tugged at his beard and smiled wanly.

'If I have your word as to your loyalty, my Lord William,' the King said quietly, returning William a reply as hedged as his own words. 'Let us then lay that matter aside and, against the possibility of your suffering from any ill-consequence engendered by my Cousin of France, I shall, from this day, restore to you all your lands and powers in the southern March of Wales and add, besides, Gower and Haverfordwest.'

'Your Grace...' William bowed his head in gratitude, but John was already contemplating the field of glories William's advice conjured up.

'With Otto in the field, we might attack the Capet on two fronts, the Emperor from the north and once in Poitou, I might...' John's voice tailed off.

'And a third if you send a force directly into Normandy, while with Papal blessing, Your Grace, the consequences could be considerable.

John sat bolt upright, raised his voice and reconvened his Court.

'Come, my Lords and Gentlemen,' he announced. 'We are pleased to speak of a reconciliation with My Lord of Pembroke and Leinster and call upon you all to bear witness. Turning to William he said: 'Your fealty, my Lord Earl, for all those lands I have and shall engross unto you by instrument this day and to which my Lords here assembled shall bear witness.'

William dropped again to his knees and placed his hands together in an attitude of prayer, whereupon John, staring round at the Court, pressed William's hands.

Immediately afterwards John called for more wine and sealed the matter with all the Court, calling in his confidential clerk and dictating the Letters Patent that formed the instrument of William Marshal's full restoration to the King's favour.

***

'By my troth, John, you have been ill used!'

'Aye my Lord, but I cheer myself that it was in your service.'

William stared at John D'Earley whose emaciated figure was but a shadow of his former fine physique. Gone were the bright eyes, dimmed by the gloom of Nottingham's dungeon, and the smile, that broad expression of a delight in life that had so heartened William, was but a sad imitation of the man's younger self.

'We must feed you John,' William said, clapping his hands upon his friend's shoulders, 'and feed you well.'

A month later and William and D'Earley had been reunited in London, whither William had gone from Dover on his way west following William de Salisbury's defeat of the French fleet off Damme. Longsword's victory had ended the spectre of invasion, the French vessels being set on fire so that the returning English spoke of the sea being aflame. Such an achievement had put King John in a high good humour, and with him the entire Court, including William. However, D'Earley brought William more sobering news, of the deep divisions that clove England's Barony from the King and which were not laid to rest by one day's success over the French. Far from it, D'Earley intimated; many were so hostile to John that they would have cheered a French triumph.

Late one evening, when William and his old friend sat late over their wine, D'Earley told William much of what had passed in England whilst he had been in Leinster and which D'Earley had gleaned in Nottingham and after his release. He emphasised the seriousness of the deep malcontent among the Barons, the majority of whom owed money to the King, had had castles and lands stripped from them by the arbitrary justice that John had meted out. Most of these men held fiefdoms in the north of England and the term 'Northerner' had become synonymous with grievance and incipient revolt.

But John's indiscriminate decisions had been handed out not just to nobles who displeased him, but to almost any litigant whose case came before his itinerant Court. In by-passing the Courts of Law at Westminster, John's capricious conduct had struck lower but increasingly influential layers of the feudal society of England and a growing alienation had been the consequence, a disaffection exacerbated by increases in taxes for John's expeditions, his luxurious state and his notorious excesses.

There were credible rumours that John had cuckolded half his Barons to which were added, for all their lack of evidence, darker tales which possessed a tenacious salaciousness that lent them a deep and believable significance when set against the revived allegations of John's personal murder of Prince Arthur of Brittany. And besides all this there circulated a persistent and damaging link between John's well-known contempt for the Papal Interdict, and the King's supposed predilection for Devil-worship.

The northern Barons refused to follow John into Poitou. Nor would they pay the scutage demanded of them for defaulting on these obligations, nor the new taxes demanded by the King's administrators sent among them to raise yet more money for the employment of Flemish mercenaries. That King John despoiled merchants of their wealth was of less consequence to the great majority of the Barons than that their own powers and privileges, their castles and lands were subject to the King's whimsy, and their women were exposed to his sexual appetites.

Beset by debt as so many were, such a situation could have only one outcome: a desire for John's removal and since, like William, many held lands south of the Channel, submission to Louis, the Dauphin of France, as overlord of England.

'They perceive it as the lesser of two evils, my Lord,' D'Earley concluded, his brow uncharacteristically troubled.

'You think me to have acted foolishly for cleaving to John?'

'My Lord, it is not for me to say…'

'God's blood, John!' William suddenly stirred, his somnolence thrown aside as he realised the full implications of D'Earley's analysis. 'Would you have Philippe's son on England's throne and see, when he dies, Louis rule over an empire stretching from the Tweed to the Pyrenees?'

'Such an empire would please the Pope,' D'Earley riposted unequivocally.

William shook his head. 'I am grown too old for these games,' he said relapsing into silence, his mind a turmoil.

After a moment, D'Earley said quietly, 'My Lord, there is a way…'

William looked up and shook his head. 'No, no, John, I cannot countenance disloyalty or even dissembling. I pray you do not entertain any such idea on my account.' Then, thinking D'Earley's long imprisonment had turned him from William and his Lord's insistent and blind loyalty to the King, he added, 'if you wish to leave my service, John, you are free to do so. God knows it has cost you much…'

D'Earley laughed, the first time William had seen his once familiar smile since his release from durance. 'No, my Lord, that is not my meaning but there is one who would, I think, ride to the opposing camp had he the liberty to do so.'

William frowned. 'Who, in God's name?'

'Your son Will.'

William was stunned. 'He has told you this? Come, tell me.'

'Not in so many words, my Lord, but he has made his inclination clear. The King's hospitality was not always pleasurable,' he added drily.

'Sweet Jesu...' William turned away and stared out of the chamber window. William was a dubbed knight banneret with a small following of his own, married to Alice, daughter of his father's old friend Baldwin de Béthune and entitled to act independently if he so wished. William might desire to have had him in his own camp but... He turned back to D'Earley.

'If the lad saw fit to join the rebels both you and I would thereby be compromised.'

D'Earley shrugged. ''Tis true there lies danger to us in such a defection, but, my Lord, there are also *possibilities*.'

'A foot in the other camp, you mean?'

'Should the King fall, yes, but if not,' D'Earley broke off and shrugged.

'My son would suffer,'

'Not if he was also useful to us...'

'Us?'

'To the King's party.'

'You mean as a source of intelligence?'

'We could pretend, even if he was as sticky about his honour as his father,' John D'Earley ventured.

William stared at his friend for a moment. 'By the Christ, John, but Nottingham has changed you!'

'It would change any man, my Lord,' D'Earley responded levelly.

William considered the matter for some moments as D'Earley poured more wine and waited. After reflecting upon the suggestion, William raised his head and said: 'As I love honour above all things, I cannot subscribe to such dissembling...'

'But if I sounded the lad out, discussed it with the Lady Isabelle...'

'Not that last,' William interrupted, 'as for the first I have no opinion upon the matter. As I said before, the lad is free to do as his conscience tells him, though he shall have neither my blessing nor my consent, tacit or otherwise. The matter I leave to you...entirely to you. He is in your charge, given you by the King's Grace. There is no need for you to hang upon my harness, John, you have a future of your own to forge and I would not stop so loyal a friend.'

Tactfully, D'Earley inclined his head and veered off the personal. 'My Lord,' he said simply, 'the King is losing control of his Kingdom. Without you he is like to lose it completely.'

CHAPTER THREE - RUNNYMEAD 1214 - 1215

'My Lord Archbishop.' William knelt before the Archbishop of Canterbury and received his blessing. Crossing himself he rose, turned to the table upon which lay a scattering of documents, beckoned Thomas to his side and asked the Primate if he desired wine. Stephen Langton shook his head. 'Then to the King's affairs,' William said briskly.

Langton assumed his seat with less haste, studying the man the King had set at his hand to deal with the present crisis. 'I have it heard said that you, like the King, are a Devil worshipper, My Lord of Pembroke.'

William spluttered into his goblet, outraged. 'By the Rood, Langton!' he exclaimed, his eyes blazing, 'I have just received your blessing, whence came this notion, for the love and hoped for desire of heaven?'

''Tis something I heard,' responded Langton unfazed, looking at the big, blustering man who, the Archbishop knew well, could neither read nor write, then studying the nails of his right hand.

'Then you should stop your ears before I box them!' William roared. 'God knows the King did not want you for Archbishop and now I am not certain that I can execute His Grace's commission with a man who traduces my honour upon our first acquaintance!'

'Have you not found there is no smoke without fire?'

'And what *smoke* have you discovered?' William snarled.

'An old story, perhaps,' Langton replied coolly, giving William a cold smile.'God's blood but you believe that nonsense that I was born with the Devil's mark, is that it?'

Langton shrugged. 'Something of the sort. Besides, you were excommunicated in Leinster by Ailbe of Ferns.'

'And have I not, like the King and his Kingdom, had Papal Interdict lifted from me by your appointment to the See of Canterbury?' expostulated a furious William.

'Not necessarily as regards Bishop Ailbe…' Langton began, but William was not listening.

'As for that infamous nonsense about bearing the Devil's imprint,' he went on, angrily, 'I bear a birth-mark that has, since by arrival into this benighted world, divided opinion amongst those who thought it mete and right to have an opinion upon my person. God alone Lord knows why a man should be judged by some blemish on his skin, any more than the irregularity of his nose, but such fancies pass for wisdom among a certain breed. Some said my birth-mark looked like Satan, tail and all, though the pitch-fork is missing, as are the horns, the pointed ears and the general stink of brimstone; others, of a nobler cast of mind considered the likeness more closely resembled a lion rampant.' William paused a moment then he leaned forward, his voice lower, sarcastic. 'That much is true. but I have to confess I am astonished that my Lord Archbishop has so great a grasp of matters spiritual that he gives credence to a tale that made women shudder and fools wet themselves, but for which there is not one shred of evidence in my conduct.' He paused, then just as Langton was about to respond, he added: 'I see you take me for a fool; so be it. But I have marked you for a greater one, for a fool without learning is merely ignorant, whereas a fool *with* learning is a fool indeed.'

'You are close to the King,' Langton said, quietly, ignoring William's insult, though the reproach stung him.

'You think that a signal of mine own unholiness?' William asked. Langton shrugged again. 'Well, Archbishop, it was not always so. Like you I have been held *persona non grata* in the King's opinion. As for His Grace's predilection for Devil-worship, I suggest you enquire of him yourself. You may find yourself in a less comfortable situation that you are now; his father, you may be too young to recall,' William added pointedly, 'had a way with Archbishops...'

'That is an impious damnable remark,' said Langton, stung and at last unable to conceal it. He crossed himself. 'Henry Curtmantle did penance for an idle remark...'

'And Becket was *dead*, Langton! In Heaven, undoubtedly, but nevertheless dead,' William said vehemently. 'Think on that, or are you so hell-bent upon becoming a saint that you stoke up my enmity that I may put an end to you, eh? Well, I am not such a hot-head as you obviously suppose. I am bound to support the King for he is the legitimate power in the land and you, my Lord Archbishop, are sworn by Papal instruction to uphold the King's rights.' William let his words hang in the air as Langton resumed his air of cool detachment, fingering the cross that hung about his neck on its gold chain and casting his eyes upon the documents laid before him.

'Well, my Lord of Pembroke, since we have cleared the air between us, shall we attend to the matters laid before us?'

William did not trouble to answer. The crisis that John D'Earley had predicted had erupted in the wine-flushed face of the King of England. His ally, the Emperor Otto and half the chivalry of Germany, had been smashed at Bouvines on Sunday 27 July 1214 by the forces of Philippe Augustus of France. The rout had had huge consequences for King John, undermining his entire strategy for the recovery of his lost hereditary lands in Normandy, Poitou, Anjou and Aquitaine, a strategy that John had, in any case, already bungled. Left in England William could only listen to the rumours that filtered back across the Channel: that after landing at La Rochelle John had made ground in Aquitaine and Anjou before sitting down and opening siege lines against the newly constructed fortress of La Roche-aux-Moine built by William's old companion-in-arms William des Roches. When a relieving force under the Dauphin Louis approached, John feared it to be the entire French army and raised the siege, ordering a retreat. King Philippe, meanwhile, led a second force north from Paris where, near Lille, a charge by the flower of French chivalry put the knights of Otto IV to flight in a spectacular and rare pitched battle, while John's half-brother, William Longsword, Earl of Salisbury and victor of Damme, had been captured at the head of his troops in Normandy.

In the aftermath of this military catastrophe, John had been obliged to concede that his French possessions were irretrievably lost – all but the Calais Pale – leaving his family's arch enemy, Philippe Augustus, the most powerful monarch in Christendom. To escape total humiliation, John was mulcted of a huge indemnity of sixty thousand marks, bound supine to a five-year peace treaty and returned home in

October of 1214 a broken man, his war-chest empty, his Barons divided and his Kingdom in dire peril, from both within and without.

From this dark hour arose the necessity for William, as the foremost of the Barons remaining loyal, and Archbishop Stephen Langton, imposed upon John by the Pope, to consider the best policy for the King.

As if no cross words had passed between them Langton, drumming his long fingers on the table, regarded William and said, 'the situation is tricky; the lifting of the Papal Interdict elevates John's position somewhat, but the Holy Father is unwilling to thwart His Most Christian servant Philippe Capet of France. I may keep Philippe at bay by diplomacy, which leaves the problem of rebellion here, in England.' Langton looked up at William, 'do you not think, my Lord, that England would be better governed by a King of Philippe's puissance, a God-fearing monarch...'

'The Barons might tell you so, My Lord Archbishop, and indeed many of them might settle for such a thing, but England would not have any of it...'

'England...?' asked Langton vaguely, frowning. 'What mean you by England, if not the person of John himself?'

'The *people* of England, the merchants in our towns and cities, they are a rising power. You have been in exile aboard too long Archbishop. Times change and John is still held to be the rightful heir of Henry Curtmantle's body.'

Langton sighed, am exasperated exhalation that William supposed indicated he considered he was dealing with a simpleton. The man's arrogance was infuriating, but William's presumption seemed correct when the Archbishop, with mock patience, condescendingly said, 'My Lord of Pembroke, England at the present moment, even by your reckoning, *is the King*.,. the anointed King. The people you speak of have no voice in the Kingdom. It is not they who are up in arms, provisioning castles, constructing siege engines and generally preparing for war unless they do it at their legitimate masters' behest. It is the Barons who oppose the King's sacred person, and it is the Barons against whom we shall shortly be arraigned...'

'You do not need to teach me my business, my Lord Archbishop,' William said curtly, 'but there are many strands that lead to the King's Grace, many pillars to his throne; one can deal with one, but must consider the others. I am surprised,' William added sarcastically, 'that a man familiar with the mysteries of the Holy Trinity denies some semblance of similarity in the power of an anointed King...'

'By the Body of Christ, Pembroke, that is near damnable blasphemy!' Langton crossed himself.

'The whole of England is in increasing uproar,' William went on blandly, pleased that he had struck at Langton and found a weakness, 'it is not our duty to ponder anything other than the betterment of the King's affairs…'

'By which your entire well-being hangs…' riposted Langton.

'That may well be the case,' remarked William with a wry smile, refusing to rise to Langton's bait and irritated that this sniping between them was counter-productive, 'but it illuminates my path most wonderfully. Now, until the King can replenish his war chest, we must buy time, hear the rebels' demands, concede some points, maintain a debate.'

Langton sighed again, though this time it was clear he was prepared to turn his attention to matters of state. Perhaps the man beside him was less of an oaf than he had both supposed and been led to believe. His son, it was said, was in the enemy's camp, but he would let that lie for the time being. 'Go on,' he said.

'The King is bringing mercenaries from Poitou, I have sent out orders for the preparation of all Royal castles to withstand sieges of up to thirty days' duration and it is my advice that we should arrange a parley with the Barons at Oxford within the month. A letter from yourself to Robert FitzWalter…'

'He who calls himself Marshal of the Army of God and the Church?' asked Langton with apparent distaste.

'The same…'

'Why do you not approach them through your son, William, my Lord? I hear he stands high in the rebels' ranks.'

William laughed and stared directly at Langton. He had been waiting for this particular accusation and was glad that it was now in the open, for he had gleaned some information through D'Earley with which to smite this haughty prelate. 'Sons are often wayward, I was myself. But if we are talking about tittle-tattle, I am informed that you yourself are not unsympathetic to the rebels' cause and would draw England under France's mantle.'

'Heard you that from your son?' Langton sneered, but it was clear the barb had unsettled him.

William refused the goading. 'A letter then, to FitzWalter…?'

***

William paced the flagstones of the New Temple in London, his nostrils assailed by the smell of incense, his ears by the drone of Langton on his knees before the altar. Two or three Knights Templar were in attendance, maintaining a discreet watch on the proposed proceedings, among them Aimery St Maur, Grand Master of the English Order. The January day was already far advanced and William grew impatient of the rebels keeping their word to meet the King's chief negotiators. A movement behind him caused William to turn. Langton had risen from his knees, drawing a bevy of clerks behind him. The chink of harness and voices came to them from without. An instant later the west door was thrown open and a score of armed and armoured men strode down the nave in a jingle of steel harness.

'What means this barbarity?' growled Langton as William, unarmed, without mail, stood his ground on the chancel steps.

'My Lords,' he said blandly, 'you are welcome…'

'Ahh, the King's lackeys,' said one whom William recognised as Robert FitzWalter.

'Do you kneel before the Archbishop, FitzWalter,' William said, unruffled. 'He would give you his blessing… My Lord of Winchester,' William inclined his head at Saer de Quincy, 'and my Lord of Essex; your father would be troubled to see you in such company…'

'I would not be in such company had the King treated me with the courtesy my father had earned me,' the young man replied. William could not argue, John had demanded an extortionate twenty thousand marks from Geoffrey FitzPeter's heir for a licence to marry. It was typical of the King's arbitrary impositions against which William could do little.

'My Lords,' he said raising his voice,' It is England's future well-being that we have gathered here to discuss, not personal grievances...'

'It is the King's tyranny we have come here to remonstrate over...'

'Aye! Aye!' The word 'tyranny' was taken up and echoed from the stones of the Templar's church.

'My sons!' cried Langton, raising his arms in a gesture of supplication for silence...'

'To the devil with you Langton...'

'Get back to France whence you came...'

'My Lords and Gentlemen!' roared William as the noise of disorder rose and, for a moment he regretted not wearing armour himself, though his sword swung at his left hip. 'I pray you are silent and hear what we have to say!'

He caught sight of his son William's face in the crowd and for a moment father and son stared at each other, then the younger man dropped his eyes.

'No!' bawled a Baron, 'do you attend to us and our demands!'

Again, the cry of 'Aye! Aye! was caught up and Saer de Quincy strode forward, to presented Langton with a document at which the Archbishop gave the briefest of glances before motioning it away with a contemptuous gesture. Robert

FitzWalter drew his sword and held its point towards the Prelate. William made to draw his own weapon, prompting several of the supporting Barons to put hands to their sword-hilts, but Langton stayed William's hand.

'Not in God's house, my Lord,' he said with a vehement conviction that had William, for the first time, regard him with something akin to respect.

But the Earl of Winchester's blade still wavered in the wan light of the ending day and he again waved forward the document so that Langton nodded to one of his attending clerks who took the parchment.

'Take it to the King,' said De Quincy, 'tell His Grace that I, Saer De Quincy, Earl of Winchester, at the head of the Army of God demand the King concedes these points touching the law as its precedent was set in the days of his father and his father's father, that our rights are upheld and honoured, our women unmolested and our fiefdoms not taxed beyond the limits of our means. Failure to grant us our rightful privileges and we shall renounce all obligations of fealty to the Lord John, appeal to the Pope and seek the protection against the Lord John's malice by an alliance with Philippe of France…'

'This is treason,' said William, genuinely shocked by the last demand.

'Come my Lord,' remonstrated De Quincy, 'the whole world knows you to have lands in Normandy for which you owe Philippe fealty...'

'But England has a greater claim upon me,' said William loftily, aware that he stood upon a quicksand such as that named for the old Saxon Earl Godwin. In truth, he was badly rattled. He half turned to Langton, one eyebrow raised in expectation.

Langton nodded, then turned to the quietening assembly of Barons. 'We will to the King and present your petition,' he said, his tone reasonable, reassuring.

William followed Langton the length of the nave to where, amid the horses of the rebels, their own mounts were held in readiness by their squires and grooms. Half an hour later they had passed into the Conqueror's White Tower and stood in the presence of the King.

John heard Langton read the entire document with mounting choler as William looked on. When Langton had finished he laid the thing aside as the King drank deep of his wine. John was obviously making a great effort to control his famously explosive temper and when he had mastered himself he said quietly: 'I shall have nothing to do with such impertinent demands.'

'It is but King Henry's Coronation charter,' William remarked, 'I beg you, my Liege, not to repudiate these terms…'

'Not at once, at the very least,' added Langton. 'Buy time, Your Grace, I beseech you.'

'How long must I eat the bread of humiliation?' growled John in that tone of voice that William knew might easily culminate in an Angevin rage.

'A month, Your Grace, perhaps two,' Langton said, like a drowning man catching at a straw.

John seemed suddenly to deflate, as though he had not the energy for losing his temper after all. He nodded acquiescence.

***

The proposed conference at Oxford in February never took place, the King prevaricating. Instead John, by way of Langton and William, gave assurances that he would respond in full by Easter Day, the 19 April. But when Easter came and went, the King burying himself in a great and conspicuous welter of devotion at Langton's feet, the rebel party lost patience. They mustered in great strength at Brackley in Northamptonshire under the banner of the Earl of Winchester, whose seat it was, and from where they directly threatened the King's castle at Northampton. From Brackley they sent word

75

that they would treat with the King's emissaries one last time and William and Langton, at the head of a small train of followers met them there on 27 April 1215.

Once again there was no agreement. Even as Langton and William returned to the King, the rebels invested his castle at Northampton. Meanwhile John had negotiated a loan from the Knights Templar and was busy sending out agents to hire mercenaries in Flanders, while William sent Edgar into the Welsh March to inform the Lady Isabelle that she and their younger children should secure Chepstow Castle. Edgar returned from Striguil with news that the Welsh Princes under Maelgwyn ap Rhys and Llewelyn ap Iorwerth were astir, ready to disturb the peace of the March.

The news drew William away from John's side for a month while he rode west and put all his castles in a fit state of defence and reassured Isabelle of the strength of his position.

'If all else fails,' he confided to his wife, 'We have young Will in the rebel camp...'

'I do not like such a game of double bluff, William,' Isabelle replied. 'I may have to choose between my husband and my son.'

William brushed off his wife's concern. 'Pray God you choose wisely then,' he said with a levity he was far from feeling. It was indeed no laughing matter; during his absence from the King's Court, the so-called Army of God and the Church moved south from Northampton and, in a grand *chevauchée*, seized London, driving John west to Windsor where, in early June, William rejoined him.

John was in a foul mood, entertaining the conceit that his house was cursed by the Devil, abandoned by Christ and that all the piety he had displayed at Easter was wasted. Conferring with Langton, with whom William's relationship had been transformed in these difficult months as both men grew to appreciate the other's skills, Langton confided that he was in secret correspondence with De Quincy and had negotiated a further parley conditional upon the presence of the King himself.

'You have wrought wonders, my Lord Archbishop,' William conceded generously.

'But how to get the King to agree, that is my present concern?'

William pondered the matter then said, 'It strikes me that were His Grace to be encouraged to confront the Barons with their infamy, he would like as not collapse if he saw for himself the strength of the opposition. He will do anything to hold onto the throne, I am certain. If you can ensure a Papal indulgence to benefit the rebels and remove them from John's vengeance, then perhaps some instrument could be drawn up from the original demands made in January, put into language that appeases both sides, whereupon a peace might be arranged that would stop French ambitions and perhaps lead His Grace to a more sober rule.'

Langton looked gravely at William for some moments, then nodded his agreement. 'I think you have something there,' he said, grasping the significance of the suggestion. Finally he smiled with satisfaction. 'You are truly a man of parts, William,' he remarked, using William's Christian name for the first time. He gave the matter a few moment's further consideration, then said, 'I will draft an instrument having the appearance of a Royal Charter, a gift from the King, but which secures those most reasonable of the Barons' demands... Yes, that might bring matters to a conclusion.'

'Let us pray to God we are right,' William added piously crossing himself, the Archbishop doing likewise.

'Think you that God works through us?' Langton asked with a wry smile, as he stood to summon his clerks.

'If he does not,' William responded, 'then the victory will go to the Devil...'

'Which God forbid,' added Langton; both men again crossed themselves.

***

But they still had to obtain the King's approval, and time was not on their side, for the Barons, having the upper hand in their rebellion, were growing restive at the King's endless equivocation. It was also necessary for Langton and William to obtain some measure of agreement prior to any formal conference, so both Edgar on the Royalist side and William Marshal the Younger on the rebels' were employed to meet between London and Windsor to exchange drafted clauses. In a feverish few days during which William, Langton and his clerks, and the two go-betweens hustled matters, the instrument conceived to bring peace to the Kingdom and save John's throne was drawn-up.

The problem of obtaining John's approval occupied the thoughts of the two chief architects of the document almost as much as the contents themselves. Langton argued that, to avoid a humiliating scene, John must approve each clause as it was tacitly nodded through by the Barons' representatives. William disagreed. Despite having conceived the notion initially, he knew in his heart-of-hearts that John would agree to nothing so detrimental to his own prerogatives and would argue every step of the way.

'Better to confront him with a *fait accompli*, my Lord Archbishop,' he explained, 'he will rage, no doubt, and call us traitors, whereupon it will be necessary to explain that we have saved his throne and Kingdom.'

Langton nodded; both men were thinking the same thing: whatever John's reaction, would he hold to the terms of the charter?

***

The confrontation between King John and his rebellious Barony took place among the water-meadows of the Thames at a place called Runnymead on 15 June 1215. It had been the clandestine meeting place of Edgar and William's son during the exchange of views on the preliminaries. It was a perfect summer's day as the two parties met. The King was accompanied by the Papal Legate Pandolpho, Aimery St Maur, Grand Master of the English Knights Templar, William himself, Archbishop Langton of Canterbury, eight other bishops, including Peter des Roches of Winchester and thirteen further Barons of high rank.

Ranged against the King and led by De Quincy, Earl of Winchester, and Robert FitzWalter, Lord of Dunmow and Bayard's Castle, were not only the greater part of the Barony of England, but a curious multitude of all manner of men, who, besides the mesnies and affinities of the greater Barons, were mostly of the mercantile classes, brought from London as a sign to John of the support the Barons enjoyed. The encounter was soured by the King's black mood in the face of such opposition, composed as it was of so many commoners. But, as William had predicted, John grudgingly conceded his agreement in the face of men he regarded as traitors, while the Barons made no secret of their contempt and hatred for the person of the King. Neither Langton's pious incantations, appeal to reason and his request for God's blessing, nor Pandolpho's smiling approval on behalf of Christ's Vicar on Earth, could disguise the ill-will with which the two parties came together.

'A mere show,' William said of it afterwards, telling Isabelle. 'No-one actually *signed* this *Magna Carta*,' he said, somewhat dismissively, 'which, despite the labour spent upon it satisfied nobody. The King appended his Great Seal, to be sure, but he did so only to emphasise that he still ruled England and that such grants and indulgencies remained in his gift.'

That evening the two parties had withdrawn, an air of sullen acrimony hanging over John's beleaguered Court as the cavalcade rode back to Windsor.

'Methinks the greatest beneficiaries of this day's work,' Langton had said drily in a low voice to William as they walked their horses side-by-side in the King's train, 'are widow women. At least they can no longer be compelled to remarry against their will, as for the rest,' the Archbishop opined gloomily, 'I doubt not that His Grace will repudiate any clause that he cares to.'

'I agree,' William had said quietly. 'He will certainly not tolerate a Council of twenty-five Barons empowered to judge his actions, though without it we should not have achieved a thing today...'

'Have we achieved anything?' Langton had asked dubiously, regarding the ominous slope of the King's shoulders as he rode ahead of them.

'A temporary truce,' William had grimly. 'Which we must maintain for as long as we are able.'

'Aye,' the Archbishop had answered.

***

That evening John gave vent to his feelings and went into a rage, aware that he had been trapped and that both his political position and the essential weakness of his character had ensured that he had had to make a show of concession over the great charter. This exhausting tirade was followed by a mood of sullen resentment which was roused to fury when, a fortnight later he heard that the Barons had arranged for a grand tourney to be held at Stamford. Thinking that the road to London lay open, he ordered an advance on the capital, only to learn that the Barons had got wind of this and moved the location of the tournament south. No-one seemed to know who had betrayed the King, but it was clear that a display of bad-faith so soon after the supposed concord at Runnymead would threaten the peace of the Kingdom. Only Langton and William knew of one final meeting of Edgar and William's heir.

Thwarted of London, John proceeded to England's older capital, Winchester, where a deputation from the Barons arrived to quiz the King as to the meaning of his move on London. In a pique, John decamped to the Isle of Wight, almost alone and bereft of the pomp of his Court. Here for three weeks he sought out the company and adopted the manners of fishermen and seamen in an attempt both to curry favour among these men and hide away from the humiliation imposed upon him by the meeting at Runnymead.

For some this seemed like a form of capitulation, a break-down into madness. Others, who knew John better, waited upon events.

***

'My Lord, the Archbishop is without and desires to speak with you.'

William sighed, rose to his feet and smiled wanly at Isabelle, nodding at Thomas. They were at Caversham, on the Thames near Reading, to the west of Windsor in a manor brought to

William upon his marriage and whither he had summoned Isabelle after the affair of Runnymead. In the few peaceful days of that year's high summer he had grown to love the place and they had talked of living there once the present crisis was over, but both knew that as long as John lived, England would be in a state of perpetual ferment and now the exchange of glances between the two, spoke with more eloquence than any words.

William received Langton in the main hall, sending Thomas for wine and offering the Prelate refreshment of bread and meat.

'You bring news, if I am not mistaken, and none of it good.'

'You are right.' Langton sat heavily, his face grey with fatigue, the supercilious gloss of his earlier self entirely worn away. The See of Canterbury, so sought after by Langton for so long, was proving to be far from the spiritual refuge he had hoped.

'I am removed from my office,' he muttered, at last.

'What?' roared William, slopping his wine, the colour mounting to his cheeks.

'And your soul is imperilled too. The Holy Father has seen fit to declare the Instrument of Runnymead dishonours the Apostolic See, besmirches the triple-crown, dishonours King

John as an anointed King and brings shame upon the people of England...'

'John went to the Pope behind our backs?'

Langton nodded. 'Signor Pandolpho got him exactly what he wanted. By concluding our agreement with the Barons he then submitted the *Magna Carta* to Pope Innocent in the full knowledge that His Holiness would declare it invalid. Now England trembles again on the brink of Interdict...'

'And where do you stand, my Lord?' William asked.

'With the accord we agreed, hence my suspension from office,' Langton replied gloomily.

'You know what this means,' William said, ruminating.

'Aye, war and more war, until England is exhausted with war.'

'It is not so much England that concerns me, I am more troubled by the French. I cannot see Philippe Augustus remaining supine in all this. He will intervene on the slightest pretext and, after Bouvines, half the errant chivalry of France and the Empire, any footloose free-lance in search of plunder and booty will feel the urge to support that Most Christian King in whatever mischief he moots...'

'You can expect the King's summons,' Langton said, brushing the crumbs of William's bakery from his lips. 'I am obliged to you my Lord for your hospitality, but I must to the

King's side. I do not wish him to know I spent too long a time with you.'

'And what then, Stephen?' William asked.

'For me? Well, I must to Rome, to plead my cause.'

'I shall miss your wise counsel after these months of turmoil,' William said simply, acknowledging the fact that the labours of drafting the *Magna Carta* had drawn the two men close and shown them not what separated them, but what they had in common.

'And I yours, William. There is much good in what we did together, let the King do what he will. Let us pray God works to preserve it.'

'Amen to that,' responded William, crossing himself, like Langton.

Langton was about to depart, but then turned, his face serious. 'There is one thing more and I know not the truth of it, but I had word that John is sending to Brabant and elsewhere for mercenaries.'

'He has not the money for it,' William replied indignantly, 'but if true it might play weightily in the balance.'

'Aye,' said Langton mounting his horse. 'Go with God, my son,' he said, blessing William with the sign of the cross. And then he was gone.

The sun had barely westered before a herald arrived from Oxford whither the King had arrived after his three week sojourn on the Isle of Wight. Summoned to join the King, William rode at once, arriving after nightfall. He was admitted to John's presence immediately. It was late and John was far gone in wine and jubilation, a man transformed since William had last seen him in a blazing tantrum reminiscent of his father's famous frenzies.

'My Lord of Pembroke,' he said with bibulous eagerness, 'you have heard the Pope has condemned the agreement the Barons foisted upon me, have you not? And that I have the Holy Father's blessing to secure my powers against their Godless acts of rebellion.'

'Aye, my Liege, this very day.'

John smiled with evident satisfaction. 'And,' he added, leaning forward with a leer, 'I have accomplished a *demarché* of great significance by this annulment. Langton is unhappy because he holds fast to what was agreed, which is only to be expected. I never wanted the man as Archbishop,' he said, his voice thick, 'and now I have dismissed him his office. I anticipate a full Interdict and excommunication of my enemies.'

William contented himself with a non-committal nod of comprehension; he knew what was coming.

'Which leaves you: Where do you stand, my Lord Earl?'

'You have no need to ask that question, my Liege,' William answered promptly. His loyalty to the King was not to John's person, but to John's Kingship and his Kingdom. He easily foresaw the consequences of allowing any accommodation with the King of France and the Papal Interdict was as certain as tomorrow's daylight, and with it all the civil disruption, unrest and unhappiness that ejection from the Church brought upon the common people. All his instincts clove to legitimacy, howsoever misapplied by John. As far as William was concerned, John's rule *must* be upheld, for an excess of power among the Barony and the involvement of Philippe Augustus in the affairs of England would be disastrous not only for England, but for William and his family – far worse option than even the Excommunication of the nation.

'I stand alongside Your Grace,' he said simply.

'But your boy does not,' riposted John, as if reading William's thoughts.

'My boy is no longer a boy, but a man with his own mind, his own mesnie and following. Your Grace will recall the fact that you insisted upon holding him hostage. It was not a thing he took lightly as many other sons of your Barony did not, which is one of the reasons…'

'Yes, yes,' the King said testily, brushing off William's intervention, 'I do not need a lecture from you about my peccant nature.' John seemed suddenly cautious, as though aware that he must guard his tongue, but the wine was not to be denied its power. 'We shall have war again.' He uttered the short sentence with an almost gleeful anticipation as though another opportunity to wage war would win back all he had lost.

'Aye, Your Grace, we shall…'

'Then we shall meet these rebels in open battle, if necessary, and defeat them.' John paused, apparently awaiting a response from William as enthusiastic as his own desire to take the field. 'And I shall need you beside me,' John prompted.

William felt a great wave of weariness pass over him. 'My Liege, you have not the means to wage war…'

'Which is why I have summoned you, William. I would have you go at once to London, to wait upon Master Aimery of the Temple, and secure me a further loan.'

'My Liege, have you not sufficiently drained the Templars of gold that they would advance more? And against what surety? I implore you not to send me upon a fool's errand. Aimery St Maur is a Godly man.'

'And he will do God's work and my bidding,' John snapped. 'I have the Pope's blessing, for the love of Christ!' John's tone was exasperated, as though dealing with a child. 'I lay at the Temple before coming hither to Windsor; rest assured you will find the Master as eager to help as the Holy Father has been to bless my cause. As for surety, once I have recovered my Kingdom, with your help, there will be a general levy to pay for this war and – be assured - my enemies will bear the greatest burden.' John shifted in his seat, his eyes watery, his speech increasingly slurred. 'Besides, I have already sent word into Brabant, Flanders, men are mustering under their chiefs... We shall forgo further adventures in Poitou...' It might have been the wine talking, but too late William perceived the trap he had been drawn into. 'You will bind yourself to my cause, my Lord, will you not?' Here now was the pathos of the drunk. 'And I shall be generous to you so that you will have no reason to regret your loyalty, loyalty to the anointed King of England.'

William sighed. 'My Lord King, I am grown grey in the service of the House of Anjou. You have no reason to doubt me now.'

But John was not listening to anything other than his own magnanimity. 'I shall spare your heir, my Lord Earl...'

William bowed his head in acquiescence, asking himself how he was going to tell Isabelle of all this.

CHAPTER FOUR - THE FALL OF THE KING 1215 - 1216

But the Countess Isabelle had gone to war before her husband. Even before Stephen Langton had crossed the Channel or William had issued his musters, she had had word of an uprising in Wales and had gone immediately to Chepstow, taking with her William's mesnie led by John D'Earley.

In obedience to the King's order William was obliged to ride to London to negotiate the loan from the Templars. Here he saw Langton for the last time as the Prelate prepared to leave England; as for William's meeting with the English Master of the Temple, only his friendship with Aimery St Maur, his personal pledges and the high esteem in which St Maur held him, secured what John wanted.

Before he left, on a sacred plea, William was privately admitted into the Order as a lay-brother. Long troubled by the imperilment of his soul in John's service, the Interdict laid upon him by Ailbe of Ferns and aware that his age and uncertainties of the coming months gave urgency to such matters, he had sought the spiritual advice of both Langton and St Maur. Keeping vigil before the high altar of the New Temple church, he made the most solemn oaths upon his knighthood that he strove to do always what was right.

As he parted company from St Maur, the Templar said, 'my Lord, I have issued a *laissez passer* for your son William. I hope that you will find him at Caversham.'

William looked down from his horse. 'Upon what business?' he asked, knowing how dangerous it was for it to be known that the two of them were in any kind of communication.

'He will explain.'

Although William returned to Caversham to find William, restlessly awaiting his father's return from London, his Countess had already gone. He would have much liked to see her familiar face; instead he stared at its pale image, reflected in the visage of his son and heir.

'What do *you* do here?' William asked, 'adding, 'right glad though I am to see you.'

'I came to warn you of the danger that lies in the west. Our party,' the younger man explained, flushing at the use of the expression that differentiated him from his father. 'Our party have raised the Welsh Princes and I come only to warn you of the possible losses our family may suffer as a consequence.'

William grunted, then asked, 'Your mother has gone to Chepstow?'

'Aye, father.'

'And have you more to impart.'

The young William seemed to be wrestling with some inner conflict before he blurted out, 'Aye, and I should not speak of such things to the King's confidant but that they touch us...'

'As a family?'

'Yes.'

'Well, go on.'

'It is the intention of my party to offer the throne of England to Prince Louis, Dauphin of France. They,' he paused, then corrected himself, 'we invoke the sixty-first clause of the *Magna Carta* and, by a Council of Twenty-Five, have already ruled John an unfit person to rule England.' William stared at his son, thinking fast, but the younger man took it for a reproach, adding anxiously: 'You would have heard of this soon enough, but it must not be known that I told you, or that I came hither to speak with you...' he paused. 'If I have acted improperly, father...'

'No, no,' William responded, putting out his hand to reassure his heir. 'Irrespective of my loyalty to the King's *party*,' he said quietly, with just a hint of irony, 'I must hold Wales and Leinster, if I can. But, Will, mark my words with care: whichever way matters fall out, you or Richard must have clear title to my Norman lands which I fear I shall never see again. However, hear also that as long as I live I shall, I *must*, cleave to John, for it is to him that I owe all my puissance and you your patrimony in England, even though I must needs die in harness to his House…'

'Speak not of death, father…'

William smiled, looking his son full in the face. 'I do, Will. I am an old man. It cannot be far-off now. All my old comrades are dead and the world belongs to men like you. I am sorry for your being held hostage but you were far older than I was when my father, God rest his soul, sent me into the camp of King Stephen and left me there for so long that I would almost have forgotten what your grandfather looked like had he not borne the scars of terrible burns and been thus made memorable…' William's voice trailed off, then he bethought himself of his duties as a host. 'Come, you will dine with me before you go, I will send for wine…'

'No father! I must go now. I have men not far away and I would not give them over-much to chew on.' Young William knelt. 'But I would have your blessing father, before we both surrender our persons as hostages to fortune.'

'You have a golden tongue, Will, like your mother, God bless you.'

William crossed himself and laid his right hand upon his son's head. The hair was soft and warm, like Isabelle's, and he felt a wrenching of his gut as he muttered the Latin blessing he had learned by rote. 'And now farewell,' he said, his voice catching as he raised Will up and clasped him in his arms. 'We are both in God's hands now.'

Then the lad was gone, leaving his father standing alone, and lonely, in the hall of the manor-house, lit by the lancing beams of a setting sun in which the dust-motes danced as if in mockery of the ambitions of men. William looked about him and unconsciously emitted a long sigh, touched by the wings of time.

***

Two days later William was again in the King's presence where all was a-bustle. His visit to London had confirmed what John had told him, that bands of Flemish mercenaries had been arriving in the Channel ports, at first in small numbers, but in a gradual accrual that suggested even the funds William had negotiated with Aimery St Maur would be inadequate to cover their employment. John, nevertheless, was again in high good humour and had summoned William only to discuss the coming campaign. Demonstrating his strategic competence as much as his political *nous* when it was required, a sober and cunning John played William like a fish.

'Well, my Lord of Pembroke,' he said with a smile, 'here is warm work for the two of us.'

'My Liege?'

'The Welsh, my Lord Earl, have had the impudence to come out of their fastnesses in Ceredigion and push their power into the southern March. Ranulph of Chester shall deal with them from the north, but I imagine you will be pleased to clear them out of your domain, and when you have done so, you will advance into England and hold it in my name. Meanwhile, I shall to Dover, where I have a force mustering and thence north, to drive the rebellious bastards before me.' John smiled triumphantly. 'We have at last Papal approval and an Interdict laid upon our enemy instead, just as I promised. We both now march under God's banner, my Lord Earl, and already fear for their immortal souls has encouraged a score or so of the rebels to seek my pardon for fear of losing their temporal lands along with their immortal souls.'

There was a malign gleefulness in John's features which both reminded William of his lineage and recalled the excesses of his life. William remembered too, the stories of the King's Devil-worship. He also thought of Langton and that, though John basked in the Pope's approval, Langton's adherence to the *Magna Carta* kept him absent from his episcopal throne in Canterbury.

It was two weeks before William, at the head of his personal escort, followed Isabelle west arriving at the great donjon above the River Wye where he learned more of the combination of the Welsh Princes. Taking advantage of the King's distraction and led by Maelgwyn ap Rhys and Llewelyn ap Iorwerth, the Welsh rebels had driven deep into the Southern March. It was as well William had bethought of his soul while in London, for the late summer, autumn and winter of that dreadful year were uniformly bad for his fortunes. He lost land to the Welsh incursion along the boundary of the entire north-western March, from Pembroke to Carmarthen, the rebel Princes striking as far south as the Gower. All William and his castellans could do was hold fast to their fortresses and watch the distant smoke rise above villages that were, nominally at least, under their protection but whose overlord could do nothing to defend.

For some weeks William lay in ignorance of the King's whereabouts, though he sent Edgar and an escort into England to maintain communications with Gloucester. There was talk of a siege at Rochester, but no certainty of an outcome. Meanwhile William despatched strong parties of knights to keep up a show of force throughout Glamorgan and some, at least, of Pembrokeshire. These were too powerful to attract attack by the Welsh but even so, the occasional messenger rode desperately into Chepstow from the west with news of dropping food-stocks in William's castles, urgent requests for relief and tales of rapine beyond the immediate fastnesses of their ramparts. Meanwhile, an ominous silence from across the twin barriers of the Wye and Severn had its own connotations.

For all his desire to enjoy an old man's simple pleasures at the side of his Countess with his younger children, William cursed his enforced inactivity. From time-to-time he himself rode out at the head of a column, leading his household knights, mounted men-at-arms, archers and foot-soldiers, on an intimidating sally, but such bold measures, if they achieved anything at all, only demonstrated his weakness as a Marcher Lord. For the most part it was necessary to direct others and his strategy could be nothing other than cautious, reactive and piece-meal. He relieved only a handful of his and the King's loyal fortresses, and only those closest to Chepstow; in doing so his quartering of so large a following upon the countryside only turned the villeins against him and the King's party. It was, William realised, a return to the dark days of 'the Anarchy' which he had witnessed as a child-hostage of King Stephen. Besides, first the autumnal rains were upon them, and then winter's snow.

But as the weeks passed news filtered into Chepstow, news speaking of the King's successes, though even this was tinged with darkness. John's achievements came at the expense of ransacking whole towns, the seizure of money and the unnecessary brutality of putting women and children to the sword in a reign of terror across England. Having mustered a powerful army of foreign mercenaries at Dover, John had crossed the River Medway and that September conducted a patient and successful siege of Rochester Castle. The fortress had been held in the name of Archbishop Langton, now considered among the rebels for his adherence to the clauses of the *Magna Carta*. During the siege John's troops had fought-off a relieving column sent by the rebel Barons and, once Rochester had fallen to his arms, the King had marched north. Deliberately skirting London he had made for St Alban's, his ill-disciplined army gaining a reputation for cruelty that increased with every mile it advanced.

The Barons' forces had quailed before this assault and withdrew northwards whilst, in the north of England, the northern Barony had invited King Alexander of Scotland to support them. The young warrior-king had occupied the northern counties of Westmoreland, Cumberland and Northumberland. By the late autumn the Scots army lay in its siege lines before Norham castle. In response John had continued to advanced northwards, spending Christmas at Nottingham while thick snow covered the country.

For William, Christmas 1215 was as miserable and wretched as had been Christ's natal day ten years earlier, after John had retreated from Normandy having lost his hereditary Angevin lands to Philippe Augustus. But for John, it looked as though the military tide had turned in his favour, though the King's jubilation was cut short when he learned that the increasingly desperate Barons had sent an embassy to Paris. Shortly afterwards the King sent an escorted messenger to Chepstow, appraising William of the situation. The Dauphin had been invited to assume the title of King of England and that Saer de Quincy, Earl of Winchester, had bowed the knee at the Court of Philippe Capet and offered his son the English Crown.

It was the culmination of William's fears and he was warned by the King to prepare to defend the south of England. Meanwhile, the King continued his advance north, laying waste every town through which he passed. Bereft of money he told his rapacious soldiery to seek their pay and their pleasure among his subjects so that, as Alexander fell back towards the border, John followed, his army plundering, raping and burning their way through Morpeth, Alnwick, Mitford, Roxburgh, Berwick, Haddington and Dunbar. Only on the approach to Edinburgh, where a sizeable Scots force had been drawn up to drive the English south of the Tweed, did John run out of energy. By now he had no money at all, and had so ravaged the terrain that his policy of sustaining his mercenaries by ordering them to live off the country at such a season was unsustainable. With over-extended lines of communication and what had become a rabble of robbers and rapists at his back, the determined show of force under Alexander could only have one effect upon John's character: his pusillanimity caused him to retreat as fast as possible.

Meanwhile across the south of England, a lesser war had been waged, a war with less burning and rapine, consisting largely of the traditional changing-of-hands of towns and castles. As he came south again, John resolved to send an embassy to Paris to plead with King Philippe not to intervene in the affairs of another's Kingdom. William and Peter des Roches, the Bishop of Winchester, were appointed to attend the French King and word came to William, then briefly at Gloucester in February, the same month that French ships entered the Thames with an advanced guard of Philippe's forces. It brought De Quincy and FitzWalter the news that Prince Louis would arrive by Easter.

The easy access the French had had to London infuriated John and he wished he had burned the city, but it was too late for such regrets. As soon as the Equinoctial gales had eased towards the end of March, William once more crossed the Channel and bowed his knee before Philippe of France.

It was an uncomfortable experience and William endured Philippe's snide observations about his divided loyalties. The King reminded William that he owed the Crown of France fealty for his lands in Normandy. William brushed aside the King's guying, claiming he came not on his own account but 'in the name of his Lord King, John of England,' who, William insisted, 'had the blessing of Pope Innocent III, in subduing a rebellion against his, John's, right to rule England.' He also pointed out that Prince Louis' claim to the Crown of England through marriage to Henry Curtmantle's grand-daughter was feeble, arguments that were backed-up by legal argument presented by the Bishop of Winchester.

Beyond his sneering remarks Philippe barely listened, turning aside and seemingly chatting to the Archbishop of Paris and Louis, the Dauphin. Only when De Roches had completed his plea did Philippe turn his attention to the English delegation, as though curious as to why a droning noise had ceased on a hot summer's day.

Well aware that their embassy was in vain, William had all the while been studying the Dauphin. Louis had something of the appearance of his namesake and grandfather, his long fair hair giving him a luck-lustre look, but he turned his attention back to the father as Philippe Augustus dismissed them.

'My Lord Bishop, and you my Lord of Pembroke, may return to our cousin and liegeman John and inform him that he had forfeit that slight claim to the throne of England that he pretends, that his Council of Twenty-five have ruled his reign tyrannous and that our son,' and here Philippe held out his right hand and drew the Dauphin closely to his side, 'shall shortly come over the sea into England.' The King paused, then waved his left hand in dismissal. William barely bowed, turned on his heel and left the King's presence.

He and Des Roches found King John at Winchester in a lather of expectation. Unusually, John was not slumped at the head of his board, slobbering over a cup of wine, but pacing up and down in a manner reminiscent of his father, Henry Curtmantle, and had been thus occupied since William's imminent arrival had been signalled from the city's walls.

William strode into the chamber and dropped to one knee, De Roches following. 'Well?' asked the King and William looked up to see in John's eyes that he already knew the answer. He shook his head.

'Nothing, my Liege. He barely acknowledged our presence and threatens immediate invasion by an army led by the Dauphin.'

'Shit!' snarled John, his face distorted by his fury, turning away and going to a lancet window where he thumped his fist into the stone sill, looked up into the cloudy sky and howled like a wounded dog. Then he turned back to face all those in attendance and, addressing William asked: 'What now?'

William had remained on his knees and said simply,' It is for Your Grace to command…'

'I ask for your advice,' John said, the words emanating imperfectly from teeth clenched to suppress anger. The answer was, of course, obvious, if John was to hold onto his throne and William saw the King's reasoning: he was, once again, testing William's loyalty.

'We must to arms, my Liege,' William said simply.

John stared round the chamber and suddenly his self-control snapped. He stepped forward, pressed his right hand on William's shoulder and roared: 'Get out! All of you! Await my decision without!'

As the members of John's Court withdrew, the still kneeling William once again felt the King's wrath transmitted to his own body. Only when the last man had gone did John release his grip on the older man's person, offering his hand to raise William to his feet.

William looked down at the King. John was several inches shorter than the Earl and, again William observed the ravages of drink and excess in John's blood-shot eyes and the broken blood-vessels that wormed their way under his skin. Premature ageing made his once handsome features sag and his hair, much reduced in quantity, was even less well dressed that the Dauphin's had been. William had an instant sinking feeling in his gut, he was tied to this pitiful remnant of a once powerful house whose future lay in John's heir a boy as young as had been Prince Arthur whom John had disposed-of so cruelly and callously; if John fell, all his own life's work would be in jeopardy, reliant only upon what young Will could salvage with the help of his powerful mother. It was not enough for William, *he* must not leave this life a failure...

'What counsel can you offer me, William?' the King asked, his voice low, his hand trembling, reaching for the stoop of wine that stood, half-full upon the board. 'The mercenaries I hired are restless for want of pay and have too close an affinity to my cousin of France to be reliable in such a situation as we now find ourselves, though I would fain meet these bastard rebels in the field.'

'No, by the Christ!' cautioned William sharply. 'We cannot risk a disaster such as Bouvines. All might be lost in a single hour. Fortify your strongest castles, my Liege,' he went on, switching his thoughts from the personal to grapple with a strategic answer that might best protect his own ambitions as much as the King's future. 'I doubt that with such power arraigned against us here in England and the dubious loyalty of our field force that we can prevent the French from landing, but a string of fortresses held in your name in territory the enemy may over-run quickly, will be a constant thorn in their side. Dover above all, Sire…'

'Aye Hubert de Burgh will hold Dover…and Windsor,' added the King.

'Aye and Windsor,' agreed William, 'and Lincoln…is Lincoln still in the hands of the Lady Nicola de la Haye?'

'Aye,' replied the King, his voice gaining conviction. 'And the Earls of Derby and Warwick are to be counted on, so too are Arundel, York and Surrey…'

'And Ranulph de Blondeville of Chester, but you do not mention Longsword, Sire,' William observed. He had heard rumours that, during the captivity of the King's half-brother John, Earl of Salisbury, the King had seduced Ela, Longsword's Countess; the Earl's loyalty was therefore in doubt. John shrugged and William passed quickly on. 'Very well, Sire. Our situation is not lost. I suggest we draw off our main puissance to the west where the greater loyalty lies in lands most distant from the power of France and from where we may launch strong and unpredictable *chevauchées*…'

'You into the Southern March?'

'Aye, my Liege, if you would have it so…'

'*You* would have it so,' the King said, a hint of wryness wrung from him as he warmed to William's confidence, a confidence the Earl himself was far from feeling.

'They are strong castles, my Liege, and many can be supplied by sea from Leinster whither I may send the Lady Isabelle.'

'Aye, Pembroke donjon is strong place I have heard, thanks to you, and Striguil…' John mused, giving Chepstow its Anglo-Norman name. 'But have you castellans capable and willing to hold them in my name?'

'My men are loyal, my Liege.'

The King nodded. It would not do to break his fragile optimism to question too closely as to whom, exactly, William's castellans were loyal.

'And what of London, William?'

'Let London go, as you did before. It is full of merchants. The City will come back to you when your arms are successful, and God grant that…' Both men crossed themselves with an 'Amen to that.' 'But your son, my Liege, above all things, Prince Henry must be sent to a place fast enough to hold him until God's will is made known by the outcome of this affair.'

'Aye.' The King thought for a moment. 'Devizes. What think you of there? The boy will be safe there, methinks, and I shall make Corfe a stronghold upon which I may fall back if it becomes necessary. That is how we shall proceed,' John agreed.

'And speedily, my Liege, for I doubt we have much time.'

***

But Louis did not arrive immediately, for in Paris Philippe was initially thwarted by the Pope's new emissary to England, the Italian Legate Guala di Bicchieri, who arrived in Paris to warn the French King of the great impiety he was about to undertake by pressing Prince Louis' weak claim to the English crown. 'England,' Guala reproved Philippe, 'was the Patrimony of St Peter,' adding that John, having repented, was deserving of and had had, Pope Innocent's blessing with the lifting of the Interdict on the King and his Kingdom. Having delivered this blow to Philippe's ambitions, Guala crossed the Channel to give John moral support, arriving at his Court at the end of April.

Although this hiatus bought William and his master time to throw men and provisions into their strongest fortresses, to remove Prince Henry into Devizes Castle and lay some measures of preparation, it proved as short-lived as William had anticipated. Encouraged by Guala's assurances, John advanced his reconstituted band of brigands to Canterbury, intending to intimidate any mooted landing. His good relations with the Cinque Ports' fleets led them to make a raid on the considerable amount of shipping gathering on the French coast, but Philippe remained undeterred, for he had got wind that Innocent III was ailing and decided to act against the Holy Father's wishes. On 22 May 1216, and despite being harried by English ships armed for war, a French army led by the Dauphin landed almost unopposed at Sandwich in noth Kent. John advanced to Dover but was there assailed by one of his fits of cowardice. He failed to prevent the enemy coming ashore in great numbers. His unpaid troops were mutinous, his following unreliable. Worst of all, the one man who might have stopped the rot was absent, far away, strengthening the Welsh March. Leaving Hubert de Burgh to hold Dover, John roaring his frustration in rage and tears, fled west

In the weeks that followed men other than William fought and manoeuvred for the future of England. Louis, arriving in person on English soil, acted as a magnet to the ambitious and disaffected nobility who, despite the Papal Interdict, had been appalled at the indiscriminate damage wrought earlier in the year by the King's army as it moved north. All now knew that Pope Innocent III lay dying and messages from Langton in

Rome indicated the influence he hoped to bring to bear on whichever Cardinal was chosen as Innocent's successor.

Consequently the Earls of York and Surrey defected to Louis' standard, as did William Longsword. So too did William Marshal – young Will – who secured the appointment of Marshal to Louis's English Court, not the least to guarantee his Norman domains. Greatly augmented by these defections, Louis, swiftly over-ran the whole of the south-east of England, taking Canterbury and Rochester Castle. He occupied London, whose citizens welcomed their new ruler with shows of enthusiasm, though The Tower of London, Dover and Windsor held out in the occupied territory.

John retreated west, briefly raising his standard over the ancient capital of England, Winchester. Louis followed, taking the King's castles at Reigate, Guildford and Farnham, hanging the wretches making up their respective garrisons. When Louis caught-up with John at Winchester, he fled, leaving two small garrisons to resist the invader for ten long days. Odiham fell to the French after a siege lasting a further week, following which Louis took Marlborough, while the younger William Marshal occupied Worcester.

During these troubled months, although active throughout the Southern March between Gloucester on the Severn and Pembroke on the Cleddau, by a great irony, William enjoyed some of the sweetest days of his life with Isabelle and their younger children. John D'Earley, Henry FitzGerald FitzRobert, William Waleran and his confidential messenger Edgar continued to be despatched with heavy escorts hither and yon, keeping supply lines open and gleaning news. No lover of the King, D'Earley maintained a communication with John as the King fell back to the west, the back-bone quite out of him. Despite this Ranulph of Chester, Lord of the Northern March, retook Worcester in an attack marked by its savagery, though young Will escaped with his life.

William's brief and intermittent idyll was threatened in early June. Llewelyn ap Iorworth had invaded Gwent and forced the local knights to bend the knee and swear fealty to him. William betook himself to horse, and led a large following out of Chepstow.

With impressive vigour William, with William Waleran at his side, struck west, missing the Welsh Prince but striking at one of his columns as it fell back from Usk. It was a rout as utter as anything in the grand achievements of his youth in the tourney. Within an hour Walleran had brought the chief of the raiders before the Earl and thrust him down upon his knees.

William regarded the man without rancour but was pitiless. If the fellow had been expecting arrangements to be undertaken for his ransom he was disappointed. 'I know you,' he remarked, you are Rhodri ap Richard are you not.' It was statement, not question and the prisoner made no reply, though he stared defiantly up at William. William gave him a look of contempt and turned to Waleran. 'Treat him as you shall his followers,' he ordered.

'My Lord?' Waleran queried, as if reluctant to relinquish his prisoner without any gain.

'This fellow has done fealty to me for lands in the Gower and beside the Loughor. One so easily torn from my side,' William said pitilessly, 'may be flung like his fellows to perdition. Put them all to the sword!'

***

All that summer of 1216 war flared across England and Wales. Prince Louis entered London in triumph and amid an enthusiastic welcome on 2 June. At a magnificent service in St Paul's great church he promised to right all wrongs and restore all properties lost to John's rapacity and arbitrary justice. He would, he swore on oath, restore all of England's traditional laws and he made a peace with King Alexander of Scotland, who began preparations to march south to catch John between his own and Louis' army. This now grew as, with the news of Innocent's death, those among the Barony who had clung to King John for spiritual reasons had less argument for doing so. Meanwhile his unpaid mercenaries and *routier*s abandoned John, either to return home or to take service under Louis' banner.

Having secured London and before marching to meet Alexander, Louis desired the securing of his communication with France and laid siege to Dover, battering the ramparts with a huge *trébuchet* brought over from Calais for the purpose. The loyal De Burgh held out against all expectations and eventually Louis threw-up the investment and turned instead upon Windsor which also put up stout resistance.

John, meanwhile, fled west to Bristol then turned south-east and mewed himself up in Corfe Castle in Dorset, where he remained two months listening to the blandishments of the Legate Guala di Bicchieri. Here, to his chagrin, John also learned of more defections, summoning D'Earley and sending him to William with orders that would bring about the great crisis of William's life.

'My half-brother Salisbury has joined the rebels, God rot his immortal soul,' the King informed D'Earley, 'And of my chief Barons, Arundel, York and Surrey have followed. Besides Earl William and Ranulf of Chester, of my Earls, only Derby and Warwick now remain loyal. Ride to Striguil and order my Lord of Pembroke to move his power to Gloucester whither I am sending the Papal Legate for his safe-keeping and cover the lands to the south and west. My Lady De la Haye is in peril and I intend taking my force thither, for if that rogue Alexander of Scotland and the usurping bastard Louis once join up, I am lost. Inform your master that I am making a *chevauchée* and if God grants my arms success I shall send for him to Lincoln or Newark.'

It was with this message that John D'Earley rode into Chepstow in mid-September and ended William's strange, spasmodic days of happiness with Isabelle. Within the compass of the day he had mustered all his own following, his whole household less the garrison of Chepstow, and his chief knights' personal mesnies who held his fortresses across the Southern March, and headed north-east towards Gloucester.

Here William found the Papal Legate, Guala di Bichieri, and the two men struck-up a curious friendship in which the one prayed fervently for the success of the King's arms and the other chafed at the lack of news. When, finally, it came that autumn, it came thick and fast, and from both sides. Edgar arrived first from London, whither he had ventured to carry messages and money from William to Aimery St Maur. Here he had learned of the hot news in the capital where Louis was losing favour. The Dauphin and his knights were known to be acting arrogantly towards the English Barons and a more sinister reason for this was revealed by William's old companion-in-arms, Robert de Meulan, who lay dying in the Temple hospital.

In fear of death and dishonour, De Meulan had revealed to St Maur that, once crowned King of England, Louis was intending to exile, dispossess or execute all those Barons who had risen in rebellion against John, reckoning them essentially disloyal and therefore untrustworthy.

'The very men who summoned him to what he is pleased to declare his rightful inheritance,' Edgar explained to a scarcely credulous William. 'Many of those under such a threat have betook themselves to think again of their enthusiasm for a King Louis of England.' He paused a moment, then added, 'though few, I warrant, will come immediately into the King's camp, some my Lord, might be persuaded into yours.'

William grunted. 'Robert de Meulan would not lie,' he said simply, asking, 'is his life despaired of?'

'It is feared for, my Lord.'

'May God have mercy upon him,' William said, crossing himself.

'There is one thing more, my Lord. The French are to some extent beleaguered, for the seamen of the Cinque Ports are proving loyal and have taken numerous French vessels, many of which bear remounts and arms.'

'Which will yield them a good harvest,' William commented wryly, rubbing his beard as he digested the news. Over the following week or so the defection of several Barons proved Edgar correct, as they rode into Gloucester seeking to make their peace, not with John, but with William and offering to serve under him.

'They believe that whatever the outcome you shall prevail, my Lord,' remarked John D'Earley with his wide smile.

As for news of the King, this filtered through more slowly. With the remnants of his mercenary Brabantine *routiers* he had once again embarked upon a ruthless *chevauchée*, intent upon punishing those Barons of the Midlands who had defected to the French. Reaching Lincoln to the mixed feelings of Nicola de la Haye, John prepared for a second raid and in October left Lincoln and struck south-east.

Thereafter all went quiet until, towards the end of the month, John's cause lay ruined in the mud of the Wash and his own gross appetites.

William had retired for the night when he was wakened and told a messenger had arrived from Newark. William pulled on a robe and an ageing knight was admitted to his presence.

'God's blood, sirrah,' William remarked irritably, 'what is amiss that you must trouble a man's sleep.' But before giving the fellow time to reply William, frowning and scratching himself realised he was vaguely familiar. 'I know you, sir, but forgive me...'

'Savaric de Mauléon, my Lord. We last met in a tourney in the Vexin...' De Mauléon growled, adding, 'you unhorsed me.'

'Did I? Then I must crave your pardon.'

''Tis no matter. I command a division of the King's Flemish troops,' the *routier* captain explained, and have come from Newark-upon-the-Trent.' De Mauléon's language had a decidedly French cast. William recalled him now, remembered too that in the wars in Normandy and Anjou Savaric De Mauléon had acquired an unsavoury name. No doubt his violent character endeared him to John, for such men, at the head of a large company of Flemish *routier*s would have no compunction in burning English towns and villages, nor of allowing his men to rape and loot to their hearts' content. Carrying out John's scorched-earth policies with enthusiasm would have made him no friends beyond the King's closest familiars and only such fellows could master the fractious rabble that constituted John's army.

Mindful that De Mauléon must have undertaken so long a ride out of urgent and dire necessity, William called for wine refreshment, asking, 'What brings you hither at this time of the night?'

117

'The King is dead, my Lord Earl.'

'Dead? By the Holy Ghost...' William crossed himself. 'May he rest in peace.' De Mauléon did not trouble himself to follow William's pious example. 'How came this about?' William asked as the wine arrived, indicating that De Mauléon should drink deep after his journey.

'Were you aware that the King advanced to Lincoln?' De Mauléon asked, wiping his hand across his mouth.

William nodded. 'Aye, and from there His Grace raided south...'

'And east,' said De Mauléon curtly, 'having burned all the possessions and farms of Croyland Abbey he headed for Lynn and Wisbeach. Here he was misled, crossing the sands of the Wash by a causeway that rapidly flooded when the tide made into the mouth of the River Welland,' De Mauléon went on, so matter-of-factly that William had trouble taking in the scale of the events that De Mauléon was recounting.

'The King was drowned?'

'No,' De Mauléon shook his head. 'The King and most of his close affinity escaped with their lives, but the greater part of the train, the sumpter horses and roncins with almost the entire baggage, including the Treasury and many men, most mine own, were lost.'

'God's blood. Then what...?' William began but De Mauléon needed no prompting.

'We proceeded to the Cistercian House at Swineshead where His Grace delivered himself of a rage before enjoying the Abbot's hospitality. Thereafter he gorged himself on new cider, pears, peaches and lampreys which, during that night brought on a great eruption and then a bloody flux such that he could not mount his palfrey the following morning. He was placed in a horse-litter and carried to Sleaford Castle where the fever grew hotter, whereupon and with great difficulty, the following day we carried him into the castle of Newark.'

William sat silent as De Mauléon concluded his sorry tale. 'With the shadow of death upon him he sent for the Abbot of neighbouring Croxton, who shrove him and administered Holy Unction until such time as he gave up the ghost.'

'And that is all?' William asked as De Mauléon fell silent, letting the implications of his news sink in.

'No my Lord, it is not all. Before his final hour, whilst in the agonies of death upon the 18th of this present month, His Grace appointed his son Henry his heir and successor, dictated a letter to the new Pope entreating His Holiness to uphold the boy's right to the throne and protect his other children. Those of us present swore upon the peril of our own souls fealty to the boy Henry and orders were issued to all castellans,

119

burgesses and every other man in the Kingdom holding office of authority to render the Prince that loyalty which they lately did by obedience to John.'

'This alters everything,' William murmured to himself, biting his lower lip and rubbing his beard as De Mauléon watched. William had the sensation that De Mauléon had him under observation, for the knight wore a curious expression, as if he was enjoying the irony of this tale of death, and the impact which it would have upon the man before him. Prince Henry was nine years old and the news of John's death would already have reached London, immensely strengthening Louis' position. With the Dauphin at the head of an army quartered in the Kingdom the future of Prince Henry was bleak. Given the opportunity, Louis would almost certainly dispose of him, just as John had disposed of Arthur of Brittany. Nor was William's own future much brighter, though he might retreat into Leinster, and he must secure Isabelle's safety, along with that of his children.

De Mauléon's eyes bored into William and, with an effort, he recalled himself to his duty.

'Did His Grace stipulate where he wishes to be laid to rest?' William asked.

'In his final moments the Abbot of Croxton asked the same question to which the King declared a great and hitherto unsuspected love for St Wulfstan,' De Mauléon said sarcastically, 'whose remains lie at Worcester…'

'Worcester,' William broke in, recovering his composure and grasping the significance of John's choice. Denied Westminster or Fontevrault by virtue of enemy conquest, John had bethought of Worcester where, in 1158, his parents had laid aside their Crowns upon the shrine of Wulfstan, the last Saxon bishop, a reformer whom Pope Innocent III had canonised in 1203 and at whose shrine John had prayed five years later.

'Aye, my Lord,' De Mauléon went on, 'even now his corpse is being conveyed there, escorted by Falkes de Bréauté, which is why you have me here to summon you thither.' William nodded. 'There is one thing more my Lord de Pembroke,' De Mauléon added, that expression of wry malice still playing about his features. 'The King named you as the only man fit to entrust with the care of Henry's person. He named you Guardian of the Realm.'

PART TWO - GUARDIAN OF THE REALM 1216 – 1219

CHAPTER FIVE - HENRY OF
WINCHESTER - 1216

' "In the first place, therefore, I desire that my body be buried in the church of St Mary and St Wulfstan at Worcester," ' Cardinal Guala di Bicchieri, the Papal Legate read the concluding paragraph of John's short will and testament. 'I appoint, moreover, the following arbiters and administrators: the Lord Guala, by the Grace of God, Cardinal-Priest of the title of St Martin and Legate of the Apostolic See; the Lord Peter, Bishop of Winchester; the Lord Richard, Bishop of Chichester; the Lord Silvester, Bishop of Worcester; Brother Aimery de St Maur; William Marshal, Earl of Pembroke; Ranulph, Earl of Chester; William Ferrers, Earl of Derby; William Brewer; William de Lacy; John of Monmouth; Savaric de Mauléon and Falkes de Bréauté …" ' Di Bicchieri broke off to look round at the men ranged about him in the chapter-house of Worcester cathedral: the Princes of Holy Church, the great magnates whose loyalty to John was emphasised by their continued presence at the side of the

King's body as it lay awaiting interment, the administrator with a talent for government, William Brewer; the lesser loyal barons, De Lacy and John of Monmouth, and the two powerful Franco-Norman mercenary knights, De Mauléon and De Bréauté.

In the brief silence the sound of the abbey's brothers chanting over John's corpse came to them as they stood, the last remnants of John's regal puissance, a fact of which they were reminded as Di Bicchieri coughed and concluded his reading. ' "And furthermore, be it known that it is my last wish that the said arbiters and administrators heretofore mentioned do provide support to my sons towards obtaining and defending their inheritance." '

The document was short and small in its appearance, evidence of the deplorable end to a sad monarch who had lost his Treasury - even his Crown - in that disastrous crossing of the estuary of the Welland.

Di Bicchieri laid the exiguous parchment aside and murmured a prayer at the termination of which all present crossed themselves. A heavier silence now settled upon the assembly, which included all the Lords Temporal mentioned in the dead King's will, with the exception of Ranulph, Earl of Chester, who had yet to arrive, and Aimery St Maur who was half-captive in London. Also present was Oliver d'Anjou, bastard son of the dead King. Each man looked one to another, none daring to take the initiative. William held his tongue, anticipating what would come but unwilling to be the first to speak of it. In the House of God and in the presence of the Papal Legate, it did not seem seemly for the secular Commissioners and Executors of John's will to be presumptuous, whatever their private sentiments. William thought again of Isabelle and the green lands of Leinster, calculating that if Louis assumed the throne the Southern March would be lost to him, but he knew in his soul that he could not abandon the boy-King-in-waiting.

It was Peter des Roches, Bishop of Winchester, who spoke first. After the Legate, he was the senior Prelate and all knew that he and William had been entrusted with John's highest diplomatic missions.

'My Lords Spiritual and Temporal I humbly submit to you all here who are charged with the late King's wishes that we seek the advice of My Lord William. We know from those present that His Grace abjured those about him to ensure that the Earl of Pembroke take charge of his son, Henry of Winchester, and always keeps him under his protection, for the Prince will never govern this Kingdom without the help of my Lord of Pembroke…'

That was untrue, William thought to himself; Ranulph of Chester had proved as loyal and was, moreover, a younger man, but Des Roches had made the late King's wishes clear.

As Des Roches' voice petered out there was a quick chorus of agreement. Howsoever each man saw his own future, whether in the minutes that William had been dreaming of Leinster, others had been considering retiring upon their lands, consolidating their positions and seeking a compact with 'King' Louis, they were all at that moment ready to pledge themselves to young Harry of Winchester, as the boy was known.

'My Lord of Pembroke?' Di Bicchieri prompted in his foreign accent.

William stepped forward, gathering his thoughts. 'My Lords, we have one pressing duty before us, to bring Prince Henry into our presence without delay. With your permission,' here William turned towards the Papal Legate, 'I shall see to the matter at once and have him brought to Gloucester as a place appropriate for his Coronation. We must also see his father laid to rest.'

'But my Lords, should we not await the arrival of the Earl of Chester?' asked Earl Ferrers.

'Aye, it would be unseemly to undertake the Coronation before he joins us,' added Derby.

This dissenting note gave rise to an outburst of vociferous controversy, the very thing that William feared and which made him dream again of Irish pastures and the silver waters of Waterford Haven. Such argument over matters of such comparative triviality would be the undoing of the new King's shaky cause and he could have none of it. He resorted to the only stratagem that he could think of, unconfirmed and possibly untrue though it was. 'My Lords,' he raised his voice and commanded silence. 'I have word of the enemy being in an advanced position. We have no time to await my Lord of Chester's arrival. If I know my Lord's mind he would not permit us to wait. We can brook no delay, for whatever reason.'

Once Guala di Bicchieri and the Prelates had come to William's support, the argument subsided and the matter was closed, but William was wary of the mood of those present at the beginning of the new King's reign.

It was sunset on that October afternoon when William despatched Sir Thomas de Sandford, the man who had had in his charge William's second son, Richard, to ride immediately to Devizes and bring the young Prince to Gloucester.

'Go quickly, good Sir Thomas, before the rat's nest of London stirs. The Cardinal has excommunicated Louis that he might not be crowned, but London being London might yet proclaim him and, either way, I should not wish Prince Harry to fall into the hands of the Dauphin. Be on your guard that you do not fall into an ambush,' he added, dissembling but putting fire into De Sandford's belly. 'There is word of Louis' men being no great distance away.'

'I understand, my Lord,' responded De Sandford grimly.

'And bring forth the Queen too. She should have been here for her Lord's interment...' William shrugged. 'Well, 'tis too late now. We shall ride to meet you on the morrow.'

William watched the cavalcade ride out within the hour, his son Richard bearing William's own standard as a symbol of De Sandford's authority. Whatever else he was, and whatever his heir's pretensions claimed, William was still the Earl Marshal of an England ruled by an Angevin King-in-waiting.

That evening John was laid to rest in the cathedral church of St Mary and St Wulfstan as he had desired, and before they retired the Council of Regency began the planning of an extempore Coronation.

***

Before dawn the following morning a large cavalcade left Worcester led by William, his household knights and those of the others charged with executing John's will. Leaving the Bishops to ride directly to Gloucester under escort, the Lords

128

Temporal moved in impressive force across the country and at Malmesbury met the young Henry of Winchester.

The boy reminded William of the so-called 'Young King' in whose service he had spent some years of his younger life and who would have been Henry III had he not predeceased his father, Henry Curtmantle. Despite his nine years, this young Henry mounted in front of Peter d'Aubigny, looked half the size William had been at six. But for all his small size, it was apparent that the lad had a quick mind, for he addressed William in extraordinarily submissive but courtly language.

At first William and all those new to the Prince thought he had been schooled in the matter, probably by his mother, Isabelle of Angoulême, but it turned out not to be the case. Henry possessed an extraordinary rapid grasp of facts and forms that went way beyond mere precocity and seemed some God-given compensation for his smallness of stature.

Having halted his own column, William rode forward, his head bared, drawing rein alongside D'Aubigny and his royal companion, and bowed from the saddle.

'I give myself over to God and to you, my Lord of Pembroke,' the boy said in his falsetto voice, 'so that in the Lord's name you may take all charge of me.' Having delivered himself of this oration he began to cry.

'My Lord,' replied William, moved to tears which started unbidden down his own grizzled cheeks, 'I have long given service to your House and I will henceforward be your liege-man in all good faith and as long as there is breath in my body to do that which is necessary to serve you...'

Upon arrival at Gloucester the loyal Lords Spiritual and Temporal reunited and fell to the planning, or rather the extemporising, of a Coronation. The first pre-requisite was to have Harry of Winchester dubbed knight, an office which William agreed to undertake.

Thus, as suitable robes and a circlet of gold were hurriedly prepared, on the evening of 27 October, in the presence of all the chivalry that could be mustered in Gloucester cathedral, William gently boxed Henry of Winchester with his gloved fist once on each shoulder and, with the dubbing over, knelt and girded upon the lad a sword that proved too large but which was soon afterwards removed so that the Prince could retire for the night.

On the 28th, ten days after his father had died at Newark, the Papal Legate delegated the honour of crowning Henry to Peter des Roches, Bishop of Winchester.

The preliminary oaths were administered by the Bishop of Bath wherein Henry promised to faithfully execute his duty to protect Holy Church, to deliver justice and protect his people both from foreign invasion and from evil laws and customs. Most significantly he did homage for his Kingdom to the new Pope, Honorius III, continuing the expedient submission made by his father, but thereby securing a legitimacy against the pretensions of Louis. The vow included the payment of the ten thousand marks promised by John.

Following this came the solemn moment; Des Roches, assisted by the Bishops of Worcester and Exeter, anointed Henry's bare breast and forehead with Holy Chrism and placed upon his brow the hurriedly hustled-up circlet of gold that must stand substitute for the Crown of England John had lost in the tidal waters of The Wash. Then, as Philip d'Aubigny lifted the boy King high above his head, the three Prelates presented Henry to the assembled Barony, pronouncing him 'King of England, Lord of Ireland,' adding the empty titles of Duke of Normandy and Aquitaine, Count of Anjou and Poitou, titles the Holy See recognised, at least for the time being.

At this the Barons shouted their '*Vivats*!' and each knelt before the awkward boy to clasp hands and do him homage by their oaths of fealty, after which the almost exhausted boy was carried off by Peter d'Aubigny to be divested of his heavy robes and prepared for the Coronation feast which was to follow.

At the banquet which followed, William sat at the King's left hand, the Legate being upon his right. Compared to the binges enjoyed by John and his father, Henry II, the Coronation feast of the boy-King was a poor affair and would have been unmemorable but for the sudden bursting-in of a travel-weary knight whom William recognised as being Henry FitzGerald, a knight banneret of his own following, whom he had last seen in Ireland.

'My Lord,' the fellow shouted without ceremony or deference to the boy-King who appeared terrified at the sudden intrusion. 'My Lord, Goodrich Castle is pressed hard by the enemy! You are requested to relieve it forthwith!'

'By the Rood!' William blasphemed, annoyed by the fellow's importunity as much as the dreadful news. Goodrich was on the Wye, fewer than twenty miles away; it lay between his power at Gloucester and the southern March and it was, moreover, one of William's own strongholds. 'Is this the Welsh?' he asked FitzGerald.

'Aye, my Lord.'

'What means this, my Lord Earl,' squeaked an agitated Henry.

'It means war comes to us, my Liege,' he responded, his voice reassuring. 'With your Grace's permission, I shall call a Council...'

Henry raised his right hand in a dog-tired gesture of assent and a moment later William saw him borne from the hall to his bed, whereupon William called for order and the dismissal of all but the men named in John's will, those arbitrators and administrators then present.

'My Lord Cardinal, I beg you to preside. I have promised my Lord the King that advice and service that I am able to render, and I am willing to take the field...'

'But you must stand as the King's guardian, take command in all things outside the charge of Mother Church as Justiciar of England,' Des Roches said in a tone that seemed to admit no argument and contained a hint of disappointment, even contempt. 'The matter must be resolved now, this night,' he urged.

William shook his head. 'My Lords, Hubert de Burgh is Justiciar of England. Stand loyal guardian to the boy I will, but for ought else, I am too old. The task is too heavy for me. Leave the decision until my Lord of Chester arrives, he is a younger man. Besides, the hour is late and there is time enough for us to sleep and think more soberly upon the matter tomorrow. I must this night take thought for Goodrich, for to have an enemy, even a Welsh enemy, at our back, is not a position I can sleep easily with. For the nonce, I need but this Council's approval that we move as quickly as possible.'

William waved aside further argument and the Council, having given its assent, broke up noisily. For William there was too much to think about, for the strategic position was altered by the presence of the enemy at Goodrich. He summoned FitzGerald, whom he had last left in Ireland, to learn more about the position at Chepstow, in the March and, most crucially, at Goodrich. When FitzGerald had finished, William rebuked him.

'Dost try and be more discreet when in the presence of the King.'

'My Lord, I fear I did not notice the boy…'

'He is no longer a boy, FitzGerald. He is, God save his soul, King of England.' FitzGerald asked his pardon, but William's mind was racing. 'How large is you mesnie?' he asked.

'I have twenty-seven lances at my back, and thirty mounted men-at-arms.'

'And you came hither with them today?'

'Aye, my Lord, this very evening, 'tis but seventeen miles.'

'They will not be tired then. I shall reinforce you tomorrow, but you are to return at once to Goodrich to clear the Welsh dogs from my land. Fall upon them at dawn and put all those whom you seize to the sword. When you have done so, return to my side. Go, get your men up and send me William Waleran, he shall come with you.'

FitzGerald withdrew and William sent for Edgar. 'Ride at first light for London and the Temple church. Convey my greetings to Aimery St Maur and tell him he is named by the late King among the Council of thirteen arbiters and administrators. Ask him for any intelligence he may have of Louis' intentions, the strength of the French and any other information you may glean from him. Do you understand?'

'Perfectly my Lord.'

'Then God speed.'

Having despatched Edgar, William turned his attention to Walleran, ordering him to rake-up a substantial muster of knights and men, both horse and foot to relieve Goodrich. He watched the two knights banneret leave Gloucester in the flare of torch-light before throwing himself down upon his bed-place.

***

The following morning Ranulph de Blondeville, Earl of Chester and Lord of the Northern March rode into Gloucester's castle-yard. Many of his following were openly resentful that matters had been carried as far as they had in the absence of their Lord, but as the Council convened an hour later, Ranulph had the good sense to approve of all that had been done.

There were few precedents to guide the arbitrators and administrators in the matter of a minority government and Peter des Roches called upon Sir Alan Basset, one of John's late household knights and a close confidant of the dead King, for his opinion. Dispensing with all formality, Basset declared what many where thinking in that desperate hour.

'By my faith, my Lords, though I look up hill and down dale, I see no man fitted for this great task save the Marshal or the Earl of Chester.'

'What say you, my Lord Pembroke?' asked Ranulph.

'My Lords, I am too feeble and broken,' William responded. 'I have passed three score years and ten. Take it upon yourself, my Lord of Chester, for God's sake, for it is your due, and I will be your aid so long as I have strength in life, and will submit loyally to you to the uttermost of my power. Never shall you command me aught by word or by writing, that I will not do as well as I may by God's Grace.'

After the brief carping of Ranulph's household knights, which might have been a bell-weather as to Ranulph's inner sentiments, the Earl's response, uttered without a second thought, came like a thunder-clap.

'Out upon it, Marshal, this cannot be! You, who in every way are above us all in chivalry, who be valiant, wise, experienced, as much loved as feared and fitted as no other to do this thing – you must take it and I will serve you and do your behests, without contradiction, in every way I am able.'

There was a second's silence and then the hall was rent by a great cheering and a thumping of the board. 'Mar*shal*! Mar*shal*! Mar*shal*!' they chanted and amid the racket the Papal Legate rose and signalled for William, Ranulph and Peter des Roches to follow him into a side chamber.

'It strikes me that whilst both of you are fitted to undertake this great office, neither of you wish for this burden,' Di Bicchieri began, 'yet my Lord of Chester is right in all things regarding you, my Lord of Pembroke. Besides the acclamation you just received, you possess such qualities and respect that I, in my capacity as representative of the Holy Father and in my desire to see a peaceable England thrive under the Holy See, do promise you, William Marshal, forgiveness and remission of all your sins if you shall take up this work.'

William looked at Ranulph, who smiled and shrugged. William recalled a hundred bloody acts he had committed, that of the putting to the sword the followers of Maelgwyn ap Rhys and Llewelyn ap Iorwerth among them. Had he not shortly before ordered FitzGerald to mete out the same treatment to all those he caught at Goodrich? And did he not still lie under sentence of excommunication by Ailbe of

Ferns? The Papal remission was a powerful incentive, attractive to a man aware of his own mortality.

'Very well, my Lord Cardinal, if I am saved from my sins, this charge befits me well,' he said. 'I will take it, howsoever burdensome it may be.'

'Come then.' Di Bicchieri led them back into the hall and announced that William Marshal, Earl of Pembroke, was willing to stand guardian to the young King.

William stepped forward and looked about him. 'Are you of one mind in this matter, my Lords?'

The chorus of 'Ayes' and 'Yeas' was unanimous, but William needed more than a brief acclamation; he was haunted by the vague spectre of dissent, even from Ranulph of Chester, whose encomium he must take at face value.

Looking directly first at Ranulph and then at the other Lords Temporal, William asked again: 'Dost any man here not wish to accept my authority in the grave matter of this Kingdom for now is the time to declare it and he may leave this Council and retire to his lands without dishonour.' William spoke loudly and clearly so that everyone heard perfectly what he was saying. 'Those of you who remain and have not yet done so, must swear fealty to young Harry, third of that name, as rightful King and in whose name, during those years of his minority that I am left by God to administer, that same loyalty to me, which I in turn have yesterday sworn to the person of Henry of Winchester.'

No-one moved, and William turned to Des Roches. 'My Lord Bishop, do you, under the eyes of Cardinal Di Bicchieri, administer such an oath which I shall take again and before you all, unto my Lord King, Henry the Third.' William dropped to one knee, causing a scrabble among the watching Prelates for the first to present the Holy Book upon which they might swear their great oath.

When all was done William addressed. 'My Lords, I do not take this office out of pride but in all humility, as of God's Grace. As to our present problems, you see the King is young and tender; I should not like to lead him about the country in my train. So please you, I would fain seek out, by your counsel, a wise man who should keep him somewhere at ease…'

'That is a decision only you can make,' put in Ranulph pointedly.

William nodded and sighed, turning to Peter Des Roches. 'My Lord Bishop, you have had some management of the King, being his tutor. It is my desire that he should reside in your care with some augmentation of your guard.'

Des Roches inclined his head. 'As you wish, my Lord.'

Mindful of his obligation to Di Bicchieri and his small army of clerks, William turned next to the Papal Legate. 'My Lord Cardinal, it is fitting that, under the authority of Holy Church as having in its keeping this Kingdom, I entrust the work of enscribing letters to all castellans, sherrifs to pay homage to the new King and also to all Barons and Bishops to attend a Council at Bristol on the 11th November. From such we may gauge the true strength of our following and cut the enemy line to Goodrich on the Avon.

'Further,' he went on, 'know you all that I have sent into London to inform Aimery St Maur of his place on this Council and to determine the true state of affairs among the French, of which I am certain he will have some knowledge that he may impart. Winter draws on and mayhap we have some time to prepare, but I would fain take the field at whatever opportunity offers if we may steal a march on Louis.'

Afterwards, as the Council members withdrew, William caught Ranulph de Blondeville's sleeve.

'A word my Lord of Chester…'

'You have no need to ask, William,' said Ranulph simply and informally, divining William's purpose. 'It is not a chalice from which I seek to drink and I pray for God's help in your office, God knows you will need it…'

William stared directly into Ranulph's eyes. 'I thank you, but how far dost the authority of guardian to the King extend? That I wage war in his name, I understand, but as to a competence beyond that compass, think you not that a younger man, a man such as yourself might the better execute the office?'

'As I said, it is not a task that I relish,' Ranulph responded.

Worried that Chester might decide to retire to his demesne, William pressed on, asking, 'forgive me from pressing the point, but your support for the lad?'

'Shall be as constant as it has been for his benighted father my Lord of Pembroke, that much I surely made clear,' Ranulph responded with some asperity and William realised he might have pushed his desire for assurance too far.

'I am truly grateful,' he concluded, his tone instantly repentant.

That evening a tired William sat late in the company of a handful of his most trusted people. His nephew John Marshal was present; Thomas his confidential clerk was to hand, having penned the message to St Maur, Master of the Templars; so too was John D'Earley and Ralph Musard, castellan of Gloucester Castle, within whose bailiwick the day's proceedings had taken place.

The news that the Earl of Pembroke had been appointed the King's guardian had that day received a great welcome from the Mayor, Burgesses and citizens of Gloucester, but Gloucester was not England, nor was 'the King's guardian' a post recognised by England. In the aftermath of a busy day William felt his years weigh heavily upon him, along with the burden of his task and the uncertainty of the future.

'Come, my Lords and Gentlemen,' he said wearily, too exhausted to make the effort to retire to his bed, 'give me your opinion or advice as to what must be done against the Dauphin and his power for, by my faith, I have embarked upon a wide sea where, cast about as I may, neither bottom nor shore can be found, and it will prove a marvel if a man such as I can carry safely into port.' He paused, glumly staring about him at their blank faces, realising that for so long they had depended upon him. 'I can promise you no more glory, for this cause is likely to miscarry. By ill-fortune this child-King has nothing with which to purchase loyalty, nothing with which to wage war, nothing at all and I am an aged man...'

John D'Earley broke the awkward silence. 'My Lord, we here assembled in your love will not desert you. Hold true to your cause – our cause – and no man can deprive you of your honour. If all others turn to Louis and you are compelled to retire into Ireland, what man could accuse you of having acted ill? Even such a losing game as may occur can only yield you honour and, think on this, if matters fall out the other way, how much greater will be your joy when you better the King's enemies.'

William regarded his most faithful friend whose broad face bore its broad grin. He felt stirred to tears, as he had at the speech of the boy-King, and brushed them aside, dismissing this unpleasant feature of his age. Drawing in a breath he nodded.

'By God's sword, John, your counsel is good and true, and goes so straight to my heart that if all the world should forsake the King, saving only myself, know you all what I would do?' William warmed to his own rhetoric and stirred in his seat, feeling his heart pumping hard. 'I would carry him from one land unto another, and never fail him, though I had to beg my bread!'

CHAPTER SIX - WINTER 1216 - 1217

D'Earley's endorsement of William's fitness for the guardianship of the King had sufficiently stirred the old man, so-much-so that he spent the greater part of the night that followed in consultation with his nephew, John Marshal, his chief Knights Banneret and John's two *routier* commanders, Savaric de Mauléon and Falkes de Bréauté.

Under Hubert de Burgh, Dover still held out against Louis, but this fortress was an isolated exception in the south-east, the loyalist power residing chiefly in the west. William Waleran and Henry FitzGerald had cleared the Welsh from their siege lines before Goodrich and although Marlborough had been taken by the younger Marshal, there was, nevertheless, a number of strongholds stretching eastwards, like pieces upon a chess-board, held by the late King's toughest castellans and constables, men unwilling to yield and who held Oxford, Buckingham, Windsor, Bedford, Hertford, Cambridge, Northampton and Ely. In Essex, east of London, Pleshey, Hedingham and Colchester remained in royalist hands; so too did Norwich, in Norfolk, and on the Suffolk coast Orford. Further north Nottingham, Newark and Lincoln – still under the gallant Lady Nicola de la Haye - maintained their resistance to the rebellious Barony and their French allies.

Having sent William Waleran, Savaric de Mauléon and Falkes de Bréauté to consolidate and reinvigorate the new King's position in the east, William and the Court left Gloucester on the 2nd November and moved first to Tewkesbury, a place once favoured by John. On the 10th they arrived in Bristol and on the following day Guala di Bicchieri presided over the first formal royal Council of the reign of King Henry III to which, by the letters despatched by his clerks, the Prelates and chief Barons of the Kingdom had been invited. Of the Bishops, all were present except the absent Primate, Stephen Langton, who was still in Rome, and the Bishops of London, Lincoln and Salisbury who were indisposed. The number of the loyal Barons stood at little more than had accompanied John's corpse from Newark to Gloucester. There were, however, two significant additions: Hubert de Burgh had travelled from Dover and with him arrived the Earl of Aumale, one of the rebel Council of Twenty-five.

Beyond acknowledging his presence, William made no move towards Aumale, though his presence was both intriguing and surprising. That it might also be treacherous, William set aside for the time being.

Naturally the Papal Legate assumed the presidency and called for silence. William watched Aumale as Guala di Bicchieri again pronounced excommunicate Louis, his French following and the English Barons who had invited him to invade England. Aumale's face remained impassive throughout, as he stared into the middle-distance. The Legate also excommunicated Wales for its own adherence to the rebel Barons' cause. Thus, having at his Coronation made the boy-King swear his oath of fealty to the Pope and thereby made his Kingdom a vassal of the Holy See, continuing his dead father's submission to Rome, Di Bicchieri added to the defence of England against an aspiring but usurping power the gloss of a crusade. At the time the power of this legitimacy seemed feeble policy, though at this point in the proceedings William saw a flicker of Aumale's eyes as the Earl shot a look at him. Perhaps the Legate's Interdiction had some influence after all. As for William he was, with every hour that passed, growing increasingly anxious as to the future. There was much on his mind: the King's youth – not dissimilar to his own boyhood, though with immensely greater consequences – the stirring of the Welsh, which could encompass much mischief, particularly within his own lands; and the motions of Louis, whose brief truce with Hubert de Burgh at Dover had allowed that worthy to attend the new King. Edgar had not yet returned but perhaps De Burgh could enlighten him.

When Guala di Bicchieri had concluded the solemn rite of excommunication, the Cardinal supressed the vocal reaction of general approval that had greeted it and moved on.

'My Lords, God's work knows no rest for his servants here upon this earth where, in expectation of Heaven, we all must strive for the path of righteousness. All of you, Messieurs, who bear arms in defence of the King and by your presence here declare yourselves loyal to the legitimate and anointed King Henry, third of that name, of England and elsewhere, know of his youth.' Before he continued in his heavily accented Norman-French, Di Bicchieri picked up a parchment from which all could see a heavy seal dangled. 'By common consent of an assembly of your peers and under the King's approval,' he resumed, 'my Lord of Pembroke has been appointed the King's guardian, but such powers as this invests him with lack some authority and therefore I beg to lay before you the King's wish that henceforth William Marshal, Earl of Pembroke, is "Our guardian and Guardian of the Realm, empowered by me, Henricus Rex, to make all arrangements, administrations and military dispositions to secure our Kingdom and bring peace to my people. He shall have powers of life and death and all acts of his judgement shall be those of Ourself." '

A brief silence greeted this lengthy assertion of William's new role, a silence in which those close to him heard him emit a long sigh. No-one quite knew whether Henry had been consulted upon this matter, though both Guala di Bicchieri and Peter des Roches assured anyone interested that he had approved 'the suggestion'. Once again the hiatus was ended by cries of assent to which William bowed his head.

Di Bicchieri gestured to William and he stepped forward.

'My Lords, most of you here forgathered know my mind upon the subject and I shall not detain you longer. I thank you for your confidence in me and beg God's help in our task. To this end I intend that my Lord Bishop of Winchester shall reissue the *Magna Carta* of last year in the name of King Henry III. Be it known throughout the land that it is His Grace's wish that such a measure, the breach of which caused the present unhappy rupture between the Crown of this Kingdom and many of its Barons, shall swiftly bring peace to the land and that the Barons now in revolt against the Crown of England shall come into Our camp at once and throw out the usurper Louis, Dauphin of France, who pretends an unholy claim to this Our Crown and Sceptre, Throne and all Our lands which we hold in Holy fief from Christ's Vicar upon Earth.

'Such a dissent among Our Barons is unpleasing to Us, We wish to remove it forever for it has nothing to do with Us.' William looked about him, catching Aumale's eye and, he thought, its gleam of approval. That these were William's words and not the King's seemed to strike no-one, such was the authority with which they were delivered. With the King in the safe-keeping of Des Roches and the Bishop so close a companion and confidant of William Marshal, William, invested in his new powers and sought the quickest possible end to the rupture with the Barons. If he could dislodge more from their adherence to Louis, then something might be done to secure the boy-King's future and fulfil the more optimistic hopes of D'Earley in his encomium of William's reputation. William had been heartened to see Aumale among their company that day; perhaps it was symptomatic of further defections from Louis' banner. But only if he came in love and loyalty, so he added as his own comments upon what purported to be the King's words: 'It is not right to put the evils of the father upon the son and those that persist in their rebellion are declared excommunicate.

'Furthermore,' he plunged on, thinking fast upon his feet, and switching again to appear the King's mere mouth-piece, 'since it has no part in Our administration and there is no necessity for its existence, the late King, having made provision for a Council of thirteen Commissioners, it is Our pleasure and wish that the provision for a Council of Twenty-five Barons be removed from the *Magna Carta* and that Our confidence be reposed in William Marshal, Earl of Pembroke, to be our right hand, and he is to make appointment such as conduce to the good governance of this, Our Kingdom.'

Having seen that copies of William's proclamation were promulgated as widely as was possible, William retired to his private chamber and sent word to see De Burgh and Aumale. He was exhausted after the delivery of his first statute of state, not the least because it had been made almost upon the spur of the moment, wrought – as it were – upon the hoof. That he must at a stroke remove the chief grievance of the rebellious Barons had been a compelling priority, forming in his mind for some days but, as he awaited his visitors, he found he had surprised himself by his eloquence and saw, in his mind's eye, a boy returning from years of exile as a hostage, admonishing his parents in the old wooden bailey of Hampstead Marshal, his illiteracy unchanged but his diplomacy and his rhetoric honed by his conversations with King Stephen as they played their games of 'knights' with their straw puppets.

Such memories came to him with increasing frequency and vividness as the months passed. 'Drawing me back to join the shades of those who have passed before me,' he muttered to himself, hearing not his own voice, but the lovely Welsh lilt of his old nurse, Angharad ap Rhys. She it was who had instilled in him a serious regard for those connecting modern times with the ancient days. He checked his complacency with a wry thought: It was a pity he had had to put so many of her troublesome countrymen to death...

It was the Earl who arrived first.

'My Lord of Aumale,' I am right glad to see you,' said William rising and holding out his hand. 'Would that more of your party had come hither today.'

'More of them will, I suspect, my Lord,' Aumale replied, 'and that even before they hear what this day has brought forth.'

'How mean you?' William asked, frowning.

'There are many who regret inviting the Dauphin and his knights into England. They bear us little love and act like conquerors. We hear daily of treacherous plans to remove us from our domains, which they intend to share out among themselves as happened after the Conqueror came. Besides such troubling rumours, the citizens of London have grown weary of the depredations of the French who quarter themselves like an army who have taken the place by siege and storm. Women are not safe and their drinking beggars belief, exceeding even our own when it may be had so easily at the point of a sword or knife.'

'God be praised, that French conduct should turn London against Louis,' remarked William, crossing himself and feeling a weight beginning to lift from his shoulders. Of course, Aumale could be a spy, spreading false tales, but if it were true, it was the best news William had heard in many a long and tedious day.

He called for wine and as Aumale lifted the stoop to his mouth William asked, 'You come in all honour, my Lord Aumale? I should take it much amiss if you dissembled.'

Aumale spluttered into his wine, lowering the goblet. 'My Lord! I protest! Assuredly I come hither in honour. Take me for a spy? In God's love, my Lord of Pembroke, show me some charity. You were no lover of John yourself. If any man were a dissembler it was you, with your son close to our party.'

William raised one eyebrow, saying without rancour but with a wry smile, 'Have a care, my Lord Earl, I am *in loco rex.*'

'And full glad I am of it,' Aumale said, toasting William and resuming his wine. 'God knows the Kingdom hath need of peace.'

'Then tell me, what of Louis?'

Aumale shrugged. 'De Burgh can tell you more than I, for I have not recently been in the French camp, but the Interdict of Holy Church irks him greatly and he has declared your friend Guala di Bicchieri an impostor and implores the Pope to lift the Interdiction from his shoulders.'

'He would achieve that by withdrawing his troops.'

'He will not do that, nor will his Daddy allow him now that London lies at his feet.'

'Ah, London, that rat's nest...'

'London's independence to trade and make money is important, my Lord, for the wealth of the Kingdom. Certainly its merchants have learned the unwisdom of their welcome for Louis, but they could not stomach John who no sooner saw a crock of gold in a merchant's hands, than he must snatch it away, just as he must have the maidenhead off *my* daughter or seek the bed of *thy* lady. The man was corrupted by power...'

'For all that, he was your anointed King.'

'Aye and for that reason we did not wish to dethrone him but to hold him to his conduct through our Council of Twenty-five.'

'Well, that is no longer necessary,' William remarked dismissively.

'A shrewd move,' observed Aumale drily. 'Yours, or the King's, or Guala's or Peter des Roches'?'

'God's,' responded William with countervailing sharpness, evoking a chuckle from Aumale.

The Earl rose and held out his hand. 'I have taken up too much of your time, my Lord. You have my word upon my probity. You are not a man I could ever match for honour but, with God's grace I shall not disgrace myself in your company. I shall remember you and your task in my prayers.'

As he waited for De Burgh, William longed to see Isabelle and tell her of the day's work, but other thoughts crowded in. FitzGerald and Waleran had yet to return from raising the siege of Goodrich and Edgar had not yet brought the latest news from London.

De Burgh waited upon him an hour later. 'A thousand pardons, my Lord Earl, I was at my lodgings when I received your summons.'

'No matter, De Burgh, no matter. What news d'you bring - of Dover chiefly?'

'It remains ours, my Lord. I negotiated a truce with Louis, for which I thanked God for we were reduced almost to eating our own dung. Happily, and to Louis' chagrin, an extension to the truce allowed me to ride hither, though Louis does not know of it.'

'Did his siege engines do much damage?'

'Aye, my Lord, a considerable amount, he has a formidable *trébuchet*, but it caused no breach, not even a slighting and he has lifted the siege and retired to London, there being so little in the countryside to sustain his army through the coming winter, though that is where, I fear, our people must find their own provision for the cold months to come.'

'God help the villeins of Kent,' William remarked dryly. 'Well, you have acquitted yourself well, messire, and I would have you remain as Justiciar if you are content to serve King Henry and myself.'

'You know my loyalty to the King's House runs as deep as your own, my Lord. We have both imperilled our souls by it.'

William stared hard at De Burgh; he had been implicated, at least by a widespread rumour, in the death of Prince Arthur of Brittany and William wondered if he referred specifically to that, or to a more general confession of his sins in respect of his military career in Angevin service necessarily steeped in blood. He himself, he recollected, had once been widely supposed to have lain with a Queen and, whilst he had enjoyed an intimacy with Marguerite, consort to the 'Young Henry,' it had never extended to carnal knowledge.

'What think you to be Louis' intentions?'

Like Aumale before him, De Burgh shrugged. The gesture threw the full weight of his position upon William with almost physical force.

'There was talk of shifting the siege engines to The Tower. Should he take the place the fat would be in the fire...'

'Canst bring me no more comfort?'

'They say Longsword is in the field in Essex, athwart the old Roman road from St Alban's to Colchester, but I am doubtful of this. However, there is a fellow whose conduct, if the truth be told, did more to persuade Louis to throw over the siege of Dover than my own resistance...'

'Oh, and who may he be?' asked William, full of curiosity.

'Oh, he is some common oick with a talent for archery and war. His name is said to be William of Cassingham and he heads a great band of rough fellows all armed with long-bows who have harried the French and stung them everywhere within reach of the forests of the Kentish Weald.' De Burgh chuckled. 'The villeins call him Willikin of the Weald. No Frenchman dare ride out even with an escort unless it be fifty or sixty men, and many hundreds have died in ambushes by these lawless ruffians.'

William sat in silence a moment, digesting all that De Burgh had told him, before asking, 'what makes a commoner like this William of Cassingham rise to support us?'

'I do not think he supports *us*, or the King; I think he cannot abide the insolence of the invader. Should you try and tax him and his merry men, I suspect he would resist you with as equal a fervour as he objects to Louis' knights plundering the countryside.'

'Yet he works in our favour...'

'Indeed, my Lord, for the time being, and is to be harnessed thus. Perhaps he may continue in this vein, in which case, God bless him; if not, then a noose may serve to bring his henchmen to obedience... My Lord, there is one thing more...'

'Go on.'

'Some of the seamen of the Cinque Ports have come to their senses too, Louis having obliged them to take service under his banner. It went down ill with them and they harry Louis' shipping in the Channel...'

'That is more good news,' William said quietly, 'added to what my Lord Aumale tells me of disillusion with Louis among the Barons.'

'I know nothing of that, my Lord.'

***

But whatever encouragement William derived from these two items of news, he did not retire that night without a dose of disaster. That very evening Edgar returned to his master and, having given William greetings from Aimery St Maur, confirmed all that Aumale had said about the excesses of the French making them increasingly unpopular, Aimery St Maur having presented William with an assessment of the situation he had observed in London. However, Edgar also brought the unwelcome intelligence that, on 6th November, even before the Royal Council at Bristol, Louis' men had compelled the Constable of The Tower of London to capitulate.

'God's blood, the Conqueror's White Tower!'

'Aye, my Lord.'

'And is there anything further?'

'Aye, my Lord. The day before I left the Temple it was made known that the Dauphin proposed to march north, to reduce Hertford Castle.'

'North, eh?'

'Just so, my Lord.'

'Who holds Hertford?'

'Is it not Walter de Godardville, my Lord?'

'Yes it is,' William roused himself. He was growing forgetful. 'One of Falkes de Bréauté's *routier* captains, I recall.'

When Edgar had withdrawn William mused on the state of affairs. All his life, he thought, had led to this moment and the decisions he would take in the coming weeks. As D'Earley had said, even so disadvantageous a position offered him limitless honour, while Guala di Bicchieri's absolution would wipe all trace of sin from his soul. At three score years and ten he could ask for little more.

But in spite of these promised glories, which few men can ever have had guaranteed before their deaths, God had laid before him the task which, peradventure, he must first undertake. He perceived in it, and its associated prize, that paramountcy of duty upon which all else depended. But duty came with shadows, and, while it might yield William riches on earth and smooth entry into Heaven, it might also produce defeat, obloquy and death.

Yet something else was nagging at the back of his head: the mere germ of a thought which he had to drag forward till it grew and shaped itself, and as it did so, his old heart beat a little faster and he began to take some comfort from it. He rose and began pacing up and down the chamber, ordering his thoughts, continuing thus for some half an hour before throwing himself down upon his knees in prayer. After a further period he rose, crossed himself and called for Thomas, his confidential clerk.

'My Lord?'

'Call me a Council of War tomorrow; summon all the power here resident, Barons and Knights Banneret.'

'Aye, my Lord.'

'And then bring hither pen, ink and parchment…'

Thomas bowed and withdrew. Despite the lateness o the hour, it seemed his master had shed ten years.

***

The purpose of William's Council of War was to assess what might be done. While the King's position was weak it had dawned upon William that it might not be entirely hopeless; if it were not hopeless, then he must create some opportunity for it to flourish. To do nothing was, therefore, not an option. His reissue of the *Magna Carta*, minus the clause appointing the Council of Twenty-five, was a political gambit of some potency, and Di Bicchieri's confirmation of the righteous legitimacy of Henry's succession gave a spiritual thrust to the young King's cause, but triumph lay in military success, and in hours of the night William had turned his mind to this.

Much would depend upon the actions of others, of course, but there were strings upon which he might play and in some of his close adherents he had men who understood war as well as any. The chief deficiency would, as always, be money. Money was crucial and there was none. John had not merely bankrupted the state but lost his Treasury in the waters of the Wash, so much would have to be raised from the country, a fact that would make the King's party unpopular – at least in the short term. William could not help that, and next morning he left Thomas to draft a declaration to raise taxes while he conferred with his military chiefs and began to put together an intelligence network, to assemble supplies and to muster support columns of troops able to raid, whilst determining the requirements of certain strategic castles.

'I have it in mind, my Lords and Gentlemen,' he told the assembly of his military commanders, 'to begin our work around Lady Day. If we can seek some modest accommodation with the enemy having the appearance of a weak appeal by offering a trade in castles, we may better our position.'

A murmur of debate rumbled round the room. William heard voices raised in dissent and spoke at once to quell any such misgivings.

'Pray silence,' he commanded, 'My Lords, we are woefully short of money. In fact we are desperate for want of it and must take counsel with this in mind. Whilst I have ordered the raising of a tax, it will take time to collect and we must disperse some force to support our sherrifs, mayors and burgesses in its collection, for it will prove unpopular. We are also short of men so that our position is unhappy. Even before we sat at Council in Bristol on 11th November, Louis had taken

The Tower of London...' An upwelling of astonishment mixed with despair greeted this news, for few had yet heard of it. William went on: 'He has now marched north, intending, I believe, to lay siege to Hertford Castle and I am proposing to concede him, by stages, a number of fortresses...' Again, dissenting voices were raised, but William raised his own. 'My Lords and Gentlemen, I would command you all to suffer to hear me in silence. You have invested in me powers that I must, perforce invoke. God knows the task before us is no light one but, partake of it with me, and honour cannot but accrue to you. Those who disagree are free to leave my side: now!' No-one stirred and after a brief pause, William resumed the outline of his strategy.

'We will secure a truce by way of conceding those castles which ill-serve us by their remoteness. Such concessions will be conditional upon their garrisons being allowed to march to our banner unimpeded and with all their arms, armaments and equipage. This will augment our main force while reducing Louis,' since he must pour garrisons into these places and restock them with stores. It will, moreover, extend his lines and further stoke a disaffection which My Lord of Aumale states is rife among the English Barons. We shall also buy time and not waste these cold months of winter, during which our tax-collectors shall do their duty.'

William stopped to let his words sink in. He could see that it was dawning upon his supporters that there might be some wisdom in the proposal, so he went on: 'We must proceed with caution, a little at a time. We are in a feeble position, it is true, but it would be wise to let Louis think we are weaker than we are, thereby preparing our way for a grand *chevauchée* when the moment is right...'

'My Lord, can we rely upon the enemy to honour the terms of any truce that concedes a stronghold and allows its garrison to go free?' It was John D'Earley who asked the question and it was a fair one. There were those who, knowing of the intimacy between him and William, thought afterwards that he had been planted to ask it, for William quickly returned an answer.

'Of course we cannot trust them, but we can send a force of some strength under the terms of the truce to escort each garrison to safety. Besides, I am informed that Kent is in arms against Louis' forces under a commoner named William of Cassingham, and the ships of the Cinque Ports obstruct free communication between Louis and his Father. My guess is that the Dauphin will be persuaded to seek reinforcements for the forthcoming campaigning season....'

'It is a risky strategy, my Lord,' someone said, voicing the thoughts of many. What possible advantage could be gained by allowing – even driving – Louis to reinforce his army beyond the fact requiring an expenditure of treasure? Was that key to the Marshal's thinking? Who knew. A low murmur began again. It was swiftly stifled by William.

'Who can wage war without risk?' he riposted. 'A withdrawal of the Dauphin may give us the opportunity we seek. Come, this is neither time nor place for cowards, my Lords and, looking round, I see none among you.'

***

The trade in castles began before Christmas. On 6th December a herald and heavy escort were sent to Hertford with orders to secure a promise from the Dauphin to allow the garrison to leave in safety. If he did so, Louis was told, he could have Berkhampstead as well. Louis agreed and Walter de Godardville was ordered to hand-over the keys.

Matters did not go as smoothly at Berkhampstead, where William Waleran had taken over as constable. Waleran at first refused to submit, causing a suspicious growling among the French that suggested this whole thing was a stunt. Word was passed back to William and the Court at Bristol and when, on the 20th, Waleran received an order with the seal of Henry himself appended to it alongside that of William's, he gave way, and marched out.

Having spent Christmas at Bristol, sufficiently distant for Louis to form an opinion that the young King's party was on the back foot and buoyed up by the risible notion that all seemed to turn upon the military opinion of an old man who had one foot in the grave, Louis moved to besiege Cambridge early in the New Year.

William now attempted to open a serious negotiation with Louis, dangling the prospect of further gains with the offer of Orford, Norwich, Cambridge, Pleshey, Hedingham and Colchester Castles in return for substantive truces and in late January 1217, with his entire power and the young King Henry in his company, William marched on Oxford. From here he sent a column to Nottingham to raise a relief for Lincoln and dictated letters of encouragement to the constables of Bedford and Northampton Castles. But in February the Dauphin, convinced of the weakness of the English King's party, took Castle Hedingham in north Essex, without awaiting any outcome of the talks. His forces then moved swiftly to besiege several of the other castles William had been prepared to negotiate the surrender of, thereby depriving the Royalists of the advantages that they might have accrued from their peaceful handover.

Many of the King's party regarded this dishonourable act as an exposure of the folly of William's policy, pointing out that the garrisons would be lost, as would any time to raise money. William was bruised by the turn of events and put a resolute face on these blows. He had not expected to succeed to the uttermost of his plan, but he had hoped to achieve a little more. The invaluable Edgar was employed passing across country to maintain contact with Aimery St Maur in London, but it seemed that the Dauphin had turned the tables on William and for all his rumoured alienation of the rebel English Barony, might yet displace the House of Anjou from the English throne.

Privately William ground his teeth in anger and frustration. He would fain have retired to Caversham, or his remote castles in Leinster with Isabelle and their three younger sons and their daughters, but it was too late for that. He was engaged in war *á outrance* and must bend his entire will to the matter.

Thus, when a courier from the Earl of Chester brought in the news that the city of Worcester refused to pay an old tax-debt of one hundred pounds the city council had withheld from King John, he was in no mood to trifle. He sent an order back to his fellow peer. After the formalities of greeting to Earl Ranulph he declared simply, dictating to Thomas: 'If this city does not yield up its debt immediately upon your again calling for it, you are to burn the place, excepting only the cathedral, and reduce it to ashes.'

***

William was sitting late one night over his wine with Peter des Roches, John Marshal, Oliver d'Anjou and John D'Earley. His confidential clerk Thomas was in attendance, drafting orders at William's desultory dictation, when Edgar arrived, hot-foot from London, bearing a despatch from Aimery St Maur. William indicated it should be handed to Thomas to read, but the Bishop of Winchester snatched it, broke the seal and began to read it to himself.

'My Lord Bishop,' William said sternly, 'you have the advantage over me as regards the matter of letters, but not power.'

Des Roches flushed, then gathered his wits and grinned with an attempt at boyishness. 'That depends upon whether you mean power spiritual, or power temporal and this,' he waved the missive, adding facetiously, 'is from a churchman…'

'Do not play games with me,' growled William, commanding De Roches to: 'read it aloud.'

''Tis but a note, my Lord, and tells us that Louis…'

'Read it!'

Des Roches flushed, perceiving he had acted foolishly, 'I beg your pardon, my Lord, I had not intended…'

'For the love of Christ and all the Blessed Saints, read it,' snarled William.

167

De Roches cleared his throat and began the preamble. Then he reached the meat of St Maur's message.

'*Know you that the Dauphin has departed London intending to pass over into France, leaving a garrison in The Tower and the city under Enguerrand de Coucy with strict orders not to leave this place upon any account, keeping open the navigation of the River of Thames. His going has greatly disappointed the Barons, FitzWalter and De Quincy compelling him to swear an oath that he would return.*

I am informed that in his passing into Kent he found that County in a state of open rebellion against his rule, the common people having risen under William of Cassingham and the sea-captains, mariners and seamen of those Cinque Ports not in French hands, making war upon French ships in the Channel. This I have from Philip d'Aubigny who, as my Lord of Pembroke knows, is presently in Sussex with an armed force loyal to His Grace, King Henry, third of that name.

The Dauphin makes no progress against this William of Cassingham, whose power melts away whenever it is challenged in open fight. I am told, though have no means of confirming it, that the Dauphin left orders for the reinvestment of Dover. As far as I am able to determine, Prince Louis wishes to seek his father's advice, the reinforcement of his forces, money and the lifting of the Interdict that imperils his immortal soul.

'Thereafter the Master of the Temple concludes his missive.' Des Roches lowered the document.

'That is more than a note, my Lord Bishop,' said William who had felt the soporific effects of the wine drain away with every sentence the Bishop enunciated. By the end he sat bolt upright in his chair, his eyes a-glitter, staring round at those in the chamber. They waited in silence. 'Well, well,' breathed William at last. Perhaps we have yet some hope.' He paused, then turned to Des Roches. 'My Lord Bishop, do you take the King back to Devizes. Oliver will escort you and I shall move some of our force south, to clear out the French alongside D'Aubigny and this William of Cassingham.' He turned to D'Earley. 'John, do you give warning of our move, the garrison to be left here I leave to you.' Finally, addressing D'Anjou, he added, 'Oliver, once the King is safe at Devizes, do you return to me.'

'D'Anjou acknowledged the instruction and William slapped his hand upon the board and stood, 'and now methinks some sleep…'

'My Lord…'

'What is it Thomas?'

'My Lord, you order regarding the prisoners in Corfe. It is unfinished.'

'Ah, yes. Then promise them their liberty upon condition that they proceed to Devizes and, before my Lord Bishop of Winchester, swear fealty to King Henry. Oliver may bring such of them willing to show their loyalty to join our power.'

The chamber suddenly stirred with activity. As the others withdrew, De Roches lingered.

'My Lord,' he began awkwardly, 'forgive my importunity…'

'Eh? Oh that. Well, it was unwise, Peter,' William said, half smiling, 'I did not begin the evening in a good humour…'

'I have partaken of a little too much wine, I fear.'

William slapped Des Roches on the shoulder. 'No matter. We have a turn of events here that may play to our cause. I may even be able to reinstall you in your See of Winchester. In the meantime, you have the King to tend.'

Des Roches bowed his head. 'God's blessings be upon you my Lord.'

'And God be with you,' responded William as both men crossed themselves.

CHAPTER SEVEN - SPRING 1217

Breaking up his winter quarters early, William marched south, making direct contact with Philip d'Aubigny only to learn that St Maur's intelligence had been flawed. Louis had not left for France without first embarking on a blazing frenzy of activity. Cheated of catching William of Cassingham, the Dauphin had marched on Rye and Winchelsea, recapturing both places before taking ship for France on 27 February. William, still some miles away at Dorking, could only curse.

Meanwhile Guala di Bicchieri's relentless preaching of a crusade deprived the English Barony of the pretension of the 'Army of God' and, according to the Papal Legate, it was the force under Philip d'Aubigny and of William of Cassingham, who were graced by a similar title. Wearing the cross upon their breasts, they mustered under the banner of the Army of Christ, a fact legitimised by the renewal of King John's crusading oath by his son.

Disillusioned with the French, worried about the future of their persons, souls, lands and fortunes, many of the minor Barons began to regret the stubbornly maintained rebellion against the new King, bethinking the option of a young Angevin monarch a better one than a cynical Capetian who would milk England to France's advantage. On his way south from Dorking, William was followed by news of a string of defections from these men, many not merely sending in messages – 'hedging their bets,' John D'Earley called them – but turning up in person, with their mesnies at their backs.

From these newcomers, eager to buy favour and ensure William kept the field against their erstwhile master, the Dauphin, William learned that Louis had promised De Quincy and FitzWalter that he would return by the end of April. Until then, William realised, the King's forces must seize the initiative and strike boldly and fast.

Sending a courier north to Falkes de Bréauté to apprise him of the situation and order him to do what he could to reinforce Lincoln and keep the northern Barons from advancing south, he turned aside from Rye. Philip d'Aubigny had escaped the town and joined William as he prepared to move westwards, bringing with him Oliver d'Anjou, King John's bastard. William also sent out several knights to demand money and victuals from the near-by towns, and to use the threat of burning if they did not comply.

'Be not over-greedy in this matter,' he shrewdly instructed them, 'I would not wish to entirely lose their hearts. Demand what is fair and be content with what they render willingly. But where they show truculence or disobedience, brook no argument. Put them to the torch.'

On 3 March William despatched Edgar and a herald under a flag of truce to make contact with his son, who, William had learned, held the castle at Knepp, some miles to the south of Dorking and before marching west he continued south, arriving at Horsham on the 4th. Here he was rewarded by the young William's response, brought by the faithful Edgar, whose intimacy with William Marshal the Younger had long been established in the days preceding Runnymead.

'Well Master Edgar?' William asked as Edgar rode into William's quarters.

'My Lord, the young Lord Marshal presents his duty to his father and requests that you might march upon Knepp where you shall find the gates open to you and besides your son, the Earl of Salisbury…'

'By the Christ!' William exclaimed, 'William Longsword is in my son's company?'

'Aye, my Lord.'

'Dids't see him?'

'Aye, my Lord, and bring you his greetings.'

'And what force can they muster?'

'I am not sure, my Lord, but the castle is small and was surrounded by an encampment. I should judge the combination of the two to be considerable.'

William slapped his thigh, ordered wine for Edgar and gave orders for an advance on Knepp, near Shoreham-by-Sea. Next day, the 5th, father and son were reunited as the younger Marshal and Longsword rode out to meet William, bringing all dissembling to an end. William welcomed both men, the one his own blood-relation, the other of the King's blood by virtue of being a bastard of John's father, Henry Curtmantle.

'It has been overlong, Will,' William murmured to his son as the younger man dropped to one knee, to receive his blessing, as he had done at the manor of Caversham two years earlier. William ruffled Will's hair and smiled at him as he rose to his feet. 'By God you have grown,' he remarked, staring at the strapping youth who, but for the lack of a scarred face, reminded William of his own father.

He turned to Longsword, also a man of great stature. 'Good my Lord of Salisbury, I am right glad to see you and trust we meet in good faith?'

Longsword also dropped to one knee, his right hand making the sign of the cross upon his breast. 'On my oath, my sword and my honour I denied John, but pledge my body, soul and sword unto his son Henry and to you, my Lord Marshal.'

174

Almost embarrassed, William quickly put out a hand and lightly raised Salisbury to his feet. 'How soon can you take the field?' he asked.

'Whenever you command.'

'Tomorrow then…'

'Tonight we should feast, father,' put in the young Marshal.

'Aye, Will, tonight we should indeed feast.'

***

For almost two months the King's forces in the south of England went on the offensive. The day following their feasting at Knepp, Salisbury and the young Marshal were despatched towards Winchester while William continued west and after a siege of ten days took Farnham Castle. He then marched on Winchester where Will and Longsword had taken the Bishop's Castle but had found the so-called Town Castle a more stubborn prospect. After recovering Des Roches' episcopal seat as he had promised the Bishop, William despatched his new allies further on a *chevauchée* that went first north to take Odiham, then south-west to Southampton and onwards to Marlborough, once taken by young Will, which fell after a difficult siege.

Meanwhile D'Aubigny was sent to take Portchester and Chichester, which, with the loss of Rye and Winchelsea, greatly boosted the King's power in the Channel. Information also reached William that Falkes de Bréauté had taken back the Isle of Ely.

It proved a whirlwind campaign but, while it tilted the balance of fortune somewhat in the young King's favour, it was arrested by the return of the Dauphin who landed, of all days, upon that of England's patron saint, St George's Day, 23rd April. However, his landing did not go unopposed as, approaching Dover, Louis was treated to the sight of the burning hutments that the French had built for their earlier siege and which had been set ablaze by the men of William of Cassingham and Oliver d'Anjou whom William has sent east to watch the Channel ports.

Louis was obliged to order his seamen to haul up to the north, pass inside the Goodwin Sands and land him and his reinforcements at Sandwich. On the following day, at Dover Priory, Louis was apprised of the changes wrought in his absence by William's offensive; angered, he ordered Sandwich burnt. On the 25th, having patched up a temporary truce with Hubert de Burgh, now back in Dover, he marched on Winchester, word being brought to William by Oliver d'Anjou who, leaving William of Cassingham in his forest, rode fast to join the main Royalist force.

Still at Winchester, William acted decisively and whilst there were those who clicked their tongues, no-one raised their voice against his orders.

'We are over-stretched, my Lords and Gentlemen, and while it grieves me to do so, my Lord Bishop of Winchester must lose his episcopal seat again and we must slight all those castles we have taken save only Farnham, where Louis presently lies and where, God rot his soul, Saer de Quincy, Earl of Winchester has joined him.'

'He will be pleading for the relief of Mountsorrel,' John Marshal opined, referring to De Quincy's Leicestershire castle, isolated and under siege by Ranulph of Chester and Falkes de Bréauté.

There followed some weeks of manoeuvring. As William withdrew towards Marlborough, Louis made for Winchester where he hoped to seize the young King Henry, only to find the place deserted of the Royalist party. Setting men to work to restore the city's two castles which had been rendered useless – slighted, as it was called – under the Comte de Nevers, Louis moved on London, giving orders to De Quincy for the raising of a force in London for the relief of Mountsorrel. However, Louis would not support De Quincy further than lending him seventy French knights and a force of archers and foot-soldiers under Thomas, Comte de la

Perche, for his own eyes were set upon Dover, where he arrived with his siege engines on 12 May.

Although it was as though nothing had changed that spring, with the Royalists returned to their weaker position, one thing had: William's intelligence network had been greatly improved because he had encouraged all his chief knights to cultivate the most active and astute men in their followings to undertake reconnaissance and information gathering sallies when raiding the countryside for money and provisions. He had also built-up a small team of heralds and couriers whose skills proved invaluable, complementing the services of Aimery St Maur in London.

Thus it was that St Maur let it be known that De Quincy and De la Perche had left London on 1 May, heading north towards Mountsorrel by way of St Alban's, while William of Cassingham informed him that Louis had sat down under the walls of Dover on the 12 May. Considering a replenished Dover safe in the hands of De Burgh, William bethought himself of the north. A junction of the French and the northern Barons, with the added possibility of the intervention of King Alexander of Scotland would be disastrous, allowing the enemy to push the Royalists west with the ever opportunistic Welsh Princes at their back. William had Thomas write to Isabelle, apprising her of this danger and asking her to throw supplies into his chief fortresses in the Southern March, but chiefly and at all costs to hold Chepstow and Pembroke, from where, *in extremis*, they might escape with the King to Leinster.

But that was the counsel of defeat. Old though he felt at times, there was something in the desperation of the hour that revived William and stirred his heart. Not for nothing had he chosen the device of that red lion rampant; not merely because it resolved the problem of the birth-mark on his shoulder, but that it bore a personal significance and he would fain have it raised high before death took him.

In early May Ranulph of Chester, concerned about the vulnerability of Lincoln which since Lent, had been under a renewed siege by a powerful French force, sent urgently for assistance. The French were commanded by Hugh, Comte d'Arras, and Guilbert de Ghent, Louis' nominee for the Earldom of Lincoln. In response, William, having left Marlborough after gathering in the garrisons of the slighted castles, had moved first towards Oxford where news of the Earl of Winchester's advance on Mountsorrel came in. De Quincy and De la Perche were said to be at the head of an army of refuse and scum, men whose bodies were nearly naked and whose discipline was non-existent, even for the times, who moved north ravaging the towns and countryside with the utmost savagery; St Alban's and Dunstable had suffered badly.

Ranulph had also heard of this advance, the horrors it was visiting upon the country running ahead of it with such colour that he supposed that the entire French army under the Dauphin was advancing on Mountsorrel and ordered the siege raised. The Royalist besiegers burnt their cantonments and siege engines and retired to Nottingham.

Annoyed at Ranulph's taking fright, William now hurried north with the young King and lay at Northampton on the 12th May, the same day Louis, far away, reinvested Dover. That very afternoon, with Henry by his side William sat in Council when a courier rode in from Ranulph, asking to speak with the Lord Guardian. Begging the King's pardon and beckoning Thomas to follow him, William withdrew into a side chamber, where the fellow informed William that not only had Mountsorrel been relieved, but Hugh d'Arras had summoned De Quincy and De la Perche to reinforce the siege lines of Lincoln. The rabble that De Quincy and De la Perche led was already astir and was, in all likelihood, already approaching the beleaguered city.

William thanked the man, ordered Thomas to give him wine and gold and stood for some moments in thought. Then he sank to his knees in prayer and, having crossed himself, rose and returned to the Council. No-one present forgot the look of stern resolution upon the old man's face as he stood and addressed them. It was clear that a moment of decision had arrived, though they were, as yet, quite ignorant of its cause.

'Hearken all those of you who, by God's Grace, are here in loyal attendance upon the person of our King. For God's sake hearken to me, for what I have to say deserves a hearing. This day we bear the burden of arms to defend our fame, and for ourselves and our wives and children, and to keep our land in safety, and to win great honour, and for the peace of Holy Church, which these men, both rebels and invaders, have wronged and ill-used, and to gain remission and pardon of all our sins, for I tell you that the enemy is at the gates of Lincoln and if that city falls, much falls with it.

'As for us, we stand between the two parts of our enemies' forces and by one blow might rout and destroy all their hopes here in the north...'

'Dost my Lord propose a pitched battle?' asked Peter des Roches, rising and standing behind the young King. A perplexed Henry looked from his tutor to his guardian as the Bishop added cogently, 'for if so, I would remind you of the fate of those who lost in one day at Bouvines all that they had striven for.'

William did not bother to agree that he was suggesting a pitched battle, dispensing with the tiresome and indecisive business of sieges and the taking of castles. It was, perhaps an old man's wisdom that he realised the war could not be won, nor Louis driven from the Kingdom and it made safe for the boy sitting confused among them without something akin to a conclusive *chevauchée*, a bringing to battle the entire force of the enemy such as they had, in miniature, essayed to achieve in the tourneys of his youth in France. But this would be no hostage taking; this would be a fight to the death of one cause or the other.

He turned upon Des Roches, then rounded upon the Council, composed as it was chiefly of his own mesnie and the mesnies of his Knights Banneret.

'For God's sake, let us stake everything upon it! This is our moment, one which will not brook delay. Remember that if we gain the victory…'

'*If*,' interrupted Des Roches.

William ignored the Bishop. 'If we gain the victory,' William went on, 'we shall increase our honour, and preserve for ourselves and our posterity the freedom which these dogs seek to take from us and, By Almighty God, we *will* keep it. God wills us to defend it! Therefore every man must bestir himself to the utmost of his power for the thing cannot be done else. There must be no gaps in our ranks; our advance upon the foe must be no mere threat; but we must fall upon them swiftly. Take heed then, that there be no back-sliders amongst us. God of His mercy has granted us this hour for vengeance upon those who are come hither to do us ill: let no man now draw back!'

A moment of silence followed William's impassioned speech, then first John D'Earley and then John Marshal raised the cry 'God for King Henry, the Marshal and England!' This was taken up by all those assembled, except Des Roches, who turned aside.

'My Lords... My Lords... My Lord and Gentlemen...' the quavering falsetto could barely be heard in the general hubbub of enthusiasm among men who did not think deeply and lived for the hour and the glory of a fight. But when the King rose and said again, 'My Lords and Gentlemen,' both Des Roches and William called for silence.

'My Lords and Gentlemen,' said the King, turning to Des Roches, 'my Lord Bishop of Winchester is, I thank God of his good Grace, tender in his feelings for me. I am grateful for his solicitude but these past weeks during which I have studied the business of war, incline me to think my father and his father would not have hesitated to do as my Lord of Pembroke suggests. My Kingdom is invaded, my cousin of France wishes to usurp my throne. How long must I tolerate being borne about in the train of an army without a victory? Hast thou not all sworn me fealty? Hast though not all proved your loyalty, and are you not weary of the lack of decision? When shall Louis not be smitten, if not now?'

And with that the boy-King sat down. Over his head William and Des Roches exchanged glances; Des Roches shrugged and William smiled gravely. The boy's precocity was winning.

'Good my Liege,' he said, 'I thank you. Our cause is just and the enemy overstretched. I am quite certain that we may achieve something both honourable and politic. Perhaps now is the moment for my Lord Bishop to bless our arms...'

William turned towards Des Roches and sank to his knees. With a rustle of surtouts the entire assembly did likewise, even the King bowed his head as he turned awkwardly in his chair. With a sigh of resignation, the Bishop of Winchester, raised the crucifix upon his breast and held it high in his left hand and with his right, made the sign of the cross, uttering a blessing upon the King's arms in Latin. Each man crossed himself and cried 'Amen, amen!' before regaining his feet.

***

That May evening the sun set over middle England in a blaze of blood red, as it had done for several previous nights, tempting the credulous and the superstitious to see it as portentous, ominous even. As the glims were brought in William and Thomas toiled over their work, William dictating orders while John D'Earley summoned the messengers and junior knights to carry William's summonses for a grand *levée en masse* at Newark a mere three days hence, on the 15th. In the meanwhile John Marshal and Oliver d'Anjou began preparing the troops then present in William's train for a rapid march on Newark, whilst maintain a security cordon around the city, to prevent word of Royalist intentions reaching the enemy.

Shortly before nightfall Peter des Roches, the Bishop of Winchester, entered the chamber. William, abstracted, looked up briefly and motioned the Bishop to sit and take wine. Concluding his dictation he dismissed Thomas and turned to Des Roches.

'Well, Peter, do I have your head or your heart in this affair, for I truly believe that he who hesitates is lost.'

'You are right, William, and you may rest assured that you have both. It will be a gamble with monstrously high stakes but...' Des Roches shrugged, 'we have not sufficient money to play and endless game of siege and *chevauchée*.'

'Exactly,' agreed William, pleased that the Bishop, whose Holy calling did not dissuade him from donning armour and riding to war, had come round to his way of thinking. But what Des Roches said next, reassured William even further, so-much-so that, after the Bishop's visit, he enjoyed a good night's sleep that night, uninterrupted by even the nagging urge to piss that had come upon him of late.

'I have something else to say, William, something closely touching our great endeavour.'

He caught William's interest. 'Go on.'

'You may recall that I once held the office of Precentor at Lincoln Cathedral. I know the city and its defences…'

'Would you have me like Gideon before the walls of Jericho?' William asked with a wry smile.

Des Roches chuckled. 'I do not say the ramparts will tumble at a blast of horns, but I know the best approach…'

CHAPTER EIGHT - LINCOLN May 1217

William woke in the darkness and, for a moment, could not recall where he was. Then, remembering he lay in a small chamber in Newark Castle, he wearily rose and searched for his piss-pot. It was the third time he had been compelled to urinate that spring night and he resented the loss of sleep, quietly bemoaning his fate, that at the age of seventy-two he had to do what a younger man would have found daunting. He quietly cursed the shade of King John, who had left his Kingdom in such a mess, and Philippe II who could not keep his greedy fingers out of English politics. But most of all he cursed Saur de Quincy, Earl of Essex, and Robert FitzWalter, Lord of Dunmow and Bayard's Castle, for their disloyalty to the boy-King of England and their making of a compact with Louis, Dauphin of France.

'Those twins from Hell,' he muttered as he composed himself for sleep again.

But he could not sleep. Within half an hour he rose again to piss and this time it was his body he cursed, for he knew that a dreadful malady was upon him, and the spectre haunted him of Henry Curtmantle, dying of an anal fistula and lying in his own stinking ordure, his very bed-chamber ransacked by his servants, his once active body lying like that of a criminal, abandoned to the crows.

William crossed himself and knelt in prayer. He was not afraid of dying; he was afraid of dying too soon, his task undone. Was that why he intended gambling the future of England upon this shaky throw to relieve Lincoln? And if it was, was this pure vanity? He rose and began to pace the chamber. The squire who slept at the foot of his bed snored the sleep of the young, but William, mindful of the need of rest for the lad, stilled his restlessness and went to the lancet and stared into the night. The night was dark and almost overcast; few stars could be seen, and them only fitfully between the drift of the clouds as the breeze blew them across the sky. A faint soughing of the wind came to him, like the sound of the wings of many small birds, as the air passed over the ramparts and out-works of the castle.

'South-west,' William murmured to himself, 'towards Lincoln.' Again he crossed himself. He was not a great believer in portents, but sometimes, in moments of personal bleakness such as this, he thought of Angharad ap Rhys, his Welsh nurse. She had taught him stranger things than Holy Mother Church. From the sky he dropped his eyes to the dark walls of the castle, its entire structure black as pitch. Beyond its bailiwick lay Newark-on-Trent, and beyond the town – England. And somewhere, out there in the shifting night lay Isabelle; was she restless? Did she sense something in the night air? She was, after all, an Irish Princess, a woman of great gifts, of a steadfast loyalty to match his own. William felt an old man's tears start to his eyes and sniffed them away with a savagery that made the squire stir in his sleep and William turn from the lancet in sudden remorse.

Stealthily he crept across the chamber and stared down at the youth. He could barely make the fellow out, but the pale oval of his face lay open-mouthed, still snoring placidly. What William contemplated at Lincoln could result in this fellow's untimely death; why was William worrying about that? Death had never worried him before; Cardinal Guala di Bicchieri would shrive the men's souls before they left Newark and no man who fell in battle in defence of the divine right of Henry III to rule England would so without being in a State of Grace. He crossed himself again and returned to the lancet. He knew he would not sleep again so resolved to turn his mind to the problem of Lincoln, to what Peter des Roches had told him, and to the notion that, having the enemy's main forces so neatly divided and Louis himself so far away, he must strike at the large *battaille* under FitzWalter and De la Perche, that lay outside the walls of Lincoln.

***

'My Lord Marshal, I desire that I lead the army. I have right of precedence after you in all affairs regarding England, even over my Lord of Salisbury who was so recently among the rebels...' Ranulph of Chester was angry. For all his unseemly display of righteous indignation, he had a point for, as he was not slow to point-out to the assembled Council of War in the great hall at Newark Castle - which still, it seemed, reeked of John's dysenteric demise - he had been as loyal to the dead King as William.

Equally angry, Salisbury, with his royal blood, was ready to make a case of this point of honour. His hand flew to his sword hilt, until William stayed him.

'For God's sake, my Lords!' William interposed himself and stood silent, until the mood had cooled.

Unfortunately, uncertain as to the timing of Earl Ranulph's arrival, William's preliminary Order of Battle had the forces mustered under Salisbury's banner in the van, but everything hinged upon the absolute obedience of all these men, the battalion commanders who stood about him now in Newark's great hall.

William looked up from the rough map that Thomas had found and had scrawled over. It showed the routes from Newark towards Lincoln. He was casting all upon a carefully devised strategy that was, withal, a wild gamble, so that this sort of nonsense over precedence was the last thing he wanted. He held his temper and declared the Council at an end, requesting only that Salisbury and Chester remained to take wine with him.

'Go to your men,' he commanded his other knights, 'check on their equipment and harness, make everything ready, for we shall march tomorrow.'

Peter de Roches hesitated, as did the Papal Legate, but William insisted they left, the one to prepare his own troops, the other to pass word that the army was to proceed to confession.

'Oh, and my Lords, do you ensure that our army is entirely equipped with the common device upon which we have agreed.' Although the townsfolk of Newark had been obliged to quarter the Royalist army for only a few days, its women had also been ordered to both feed the soldiers and sew white crosses upon all surtouts, or produce white cloth in sufficient quantities to furnish distinguishing arm-bands for the common soldiery. Apart from assisting in the identification of friend from foe in the confusion of battle, such a measure gave each man the sense of belonging to something stronger than himself, a crusader against the wickedness of the enemy.

But the army William commanded was not large. He had hoped, however, that its lack of numbers would be made up by the steadfastness of its constituent parts, so to have Ranulph, Earl of Chester, declaring so publicly an animus against William, Earl of Salisbury, was a major threat to his attempts at unity.

When the hall had been cleared, William turned to Salisbury and Chester. 'Now, my Lords, under the good providence of God this affair has been entrusted to me and I can have neither bickering nor rivalry. The outcome of our enterprise rests wholly upon God, and your good sense, as God's agents upon this earth. Therefore I pray you not to jeopardise God's works by unholy pride, resentment, or the evocation of past follies. We come together in love to work our miracle and, to satisfy our honour. The King will be generous when we prevail. I therefore offer you two alternatives: you submit to my order, or draw lots for the positions of your battalions. Thereafter I require your oaths on your obedience. Agreed? Longsword?'

William threw the first declaration at William, Earl of Salisbury, using his nick-name, to indicate that he, William, took no notice of Salisbury's previous siding with the rebels.

Salisbury took the hint nodded and growled in the affirmative. 'I am content, Marshal. Whichever best please my Lord of Chester,' he added. William turned to Chester. 'Well Ranulph?'

'I'll abide by chance.'

William drew a mark from his pouch, palmed it and held out two clenched fists. 'Since you must either submit or hold your position, Longsword, you should choose first.' Longsword chose the right; William revealed it was empty.

This piece of puerile nonsense over, both men seemed quite content to co-operate. Honour was satisfied and they gave undertakings to quarrel no further quite willingly as William reminded them that circumstances might change and with them their respective dispositions.

'Now, my Lords, I do not think we can delay further,' he went on. 'Despite our placing this place under strict curfew, word of our approach is bound to reach the enemy, so I do not intend to take the direct route along the Fosse Way, but along the line of the Trent...'

After the two Earls had left him D'Earley came in, requesting to speak to William.

'What is it, John?'

'My Lord, as you asked, I have done my best to close the road to Lincoln. As far as I can tell, only the two couriers you sent thither to communicate to the Lady Nicola have passed into the city, but I cannot be certain.'

'No, of course you cannot, that is why I have brooked any delay,' William smiledwearily. 'I am feeling my age, John. You know my intentions?'

'Aye, my Lord.'

'As do the battalion commanders. Should I fall, dost see to the matter.'

'Aye, my Lord,' D'Earley repeated, then seemed to hesitate as William turned away to dictate a letter for Isabelle to Thomas.

D'Earley coughed.

'There is something else?' William asked.

'Aye, my Lord. If it please you, I would carry your banner.'

William was on the point of refusing, thinking that D'Earley should lead his own mesnie, but it formed part of William's battalion and would be readily to hand. He smiled at D'Earley's broad, open and honest features. 'That would give me great comfort John. I thank you.' Strangely William found D'Earley's grin of satisfaction filled his heart with a sudden confidence.

***

William nodded at D'Earley. 'To horse!'

William settled in his saddle. It was early, not yet full daylight, on Saturday 20th May, less than four hours since midnight. Before they left Newark the previous day, Guala di Bicchieri had celebrated Mass and once again formally excommunicated Prince Louis, declaring the Loyalist army was truly that 'of God' as much as of King Henry. He promised them victory by Pentecost. As the army had marched out of the town, William had ridden up to the Cardinal, now on horseback, the young King Henry beside him, with an escort at their back to see them safely to Nottingham where they would await the outcome of events.

William had kicked his destrier forward, approached the Cardinal, genuflected and bowed his head. Beside him D'Earley had lowered the green and white banner with its red lion, rampant, as the Papal Legate had given him his blessing, making the sign of the cross over William and his standard. Then William had turned to the King.

'My Liege,' he had bowed again, his horse stirring uneasily under William's tight bridling. The King had been riding a bay mare and she seemed to be in heat.

'God go with you my Lord Marshal,' the lad had said, 'and bring success upon our arms.'

'Amen to that,' William had responded, then, as the King and Cardinal turned their horses south-west, towards

Nottingham, William had ridden out in the opposite direction to review his army as they began the advance on Lincoln.

As each battalion passed him, William had traversed its length, exhorting his men. Under seventeen experienced loyal Barons, four hundred and six knights had mustered at Newark and had been divided between the four battalions that constituted the Royal army. According to their status, each had a mesnie which largely consisted of mounted sergeants and men-at-arms, the whole force being stiffened by three hundred cross-bowmen who had formed an advanced guard led by Falkes de Bréauté. These too were mounted and were stationed about a mile ahead of the main body, the van of which was commanded by Ranulph, Earl of Chester. William's son and namesake, with William's nephew, John Marshal, had led out the second battalion, making way for his father when William had completed his review. Salisbury's men followed, with those of Peter des Roches bringing up the rear.

Behind the Bishop of Winchester's battalion, with a light guard under Sir Alan Basset, William's advocate as the King's guardian, came the sumpter horses, the creaking wagons, the laden roncins, and a handful of women. Some were the churched wives of sergeants-at-arms, women who would act as nurses to the wounded, but the majority were mere drabs;

all, however, were sisters-in-war and carried knives. There were no siege engines but, to avoid confusion, with the exception of the standards of the leaders of the battalions, all other Barons and knights had been ordered to leave their banners in the baggage train. Unwilling not to have their personal devices present in whatever might befall, many of them had had their staves lashed upright and their bright emblazoned fields left to blow in the breeze.

Regarding the women sitting on the wagons, some few on nags and sumpter horses, under this panoply of heraldic devices, John D'Earley had quipped that they frightened him more than the men.

'What? If you were one of the enemy, or if you were wounded and had to submit to their ministrations?' William asked.

'Either, my Lord.'

William had grunted, then spurred his horse, overtaking the column as it rode alongside the broad River Trent. Behind him he had heard the jingle of harness, the dull thud of horse-hooves on the damp sod and the flutter of his standard in the wind of their advance as D'Earley and his guard rode close upon his destrier's haunches.

William had drawn rein and ridden for a while with Des Roches. The Bishop had exchanged his cope and mitre for a

197

coat of mail and a steel helm, and his crozier for a lance. Like all the Barons, knights and sergeants-at-arms, he wore a cross upon his breast and back. For few moments they had maintained a desultory conversation, then William had remarked: 'It is deeds now, Peter, we have dwelt on words over-long.'

'Aye,' The two men exchanged meaningful glances. The entire enterprise hinged upon two factors: the intelligence that the main body of the enemy lay to the south of the city, and a notion mooted by Des Roches and seized by William – a march along the line of the Trent, and an attack from the north-west.

***

The Trent flows north from Newark to its confluence with the Humber; Lincoln stands upon the Witham, which flows east, then south into the Wash and – in general - the entire locality is flat, seamed by watercourses and ditches, arable land known as Lindsey that also included areas of marsh, water-meadow and wet grazing. Two roads led to Lincoln from the southwards, the ancient Fosse Way from the south-west, and the old Roman road, Ermine Street, directly from the south.

Under its gallant chatelaine, the Lady Nicola de la Haye, the city of Lincoln proved an exception, standing high above the surrounding countryside at the distal point of Lincoln Edge. Walled, its upper curtilage contained the cathedral and castle, the former in its eastern part, the castle an integral part of the western wall of the city. The lower town, clinging to the southern slopes of the eminence and abutting the Witham, offered the best entry to a besieging force. Here Ermine Street passed through the southern gate, turned briefly into the city's High Street and climbed the hill upon which stood both castle and cathedral, before emerging through the northern gate and resuming its former identity. This lower town had already been penetrated by the Anglo-French army.

To avoid an obvious approach up either the Roman road or the Fosse Way, a relieving force could take advantage of Lincoln Edge, the ridge of which – running from the north-west to the south-east - led directly to the west-wall of the castle, and the southern slope of which gave some measure of protection, while the gentler slope to the north enabled the army to deploy to its left unseen by the enemy, even when it had detected the presence of hostile forces riding along the ridge.

As the Royalists mounted up in the May twilight of that Saturday morning, William altered his dispositions for the coming battle. Anticipating a mounted attack over the firm and open ground of the Edge, he now placed Des Roches in command of the cross-bowmen with orders to draw his charges out in extended order. They were instructed to use their weapons with care and strike at any charging knight, if possible from his unshielded side. William also ordered two hundred of his mounted men-at-arms to be ready to kill or hamstring their own mounts, to form an instant obstacle to the enemy, horses being reluctant to trample their own kind in a *mêlée*. Falkes de Bréauté, now in command of the Bishop's division, would join William and Longsword in the centre of the English line, leaving Ranulph of Chester to form up on the left.

As the army closed with its objective, William again rode up and down the battalions, encouraging his men, shouting at them that they: 'Be of good cheer! God has delivered the enemy into our hands! Let us hasten to fall upon them, for now is the hour!'

***

The ancient city of Lincoln had been under intermittent siege for two years. In the most recent investment, it had endured three months of continuous blockade and the newly arrived forces of Quincy, FitzWalter and De la Perche had ravaged the surrounding countryside for victuals and firewood. These rough routiers were bound to be encountered and, as the Royalists began the ascent of Lincoln Edge, their scouts made them aware of enemy horsemen in the offing, a fact which when reported to William simply made him urge his forces on at an increased pace.

'At all costs,' he growled anxiously, 'we must not lose the initiative.'

William's use of Lincoln Edge to both cover and facilitate his approach and thereafter to gain a favourable tactical position had been at the suggestion of Des Roches, and at first it seemed as though the ruse had worked. As they gained height and the view of the city and its environs, they saw below the magnificent cathedral the colourful swirl of mounted chivalry, and the duller eddies of mounted men-at-arms, forming up. They saw too the siege lines and their engines, which encircled the city.

William despatched his squires to the other battalion commanders as they drew out their men from line-of-march to array, verifying that they knew the enemy were aware of their presence and to ready themselves for the shock of battle.

'My Lord, they retire!' John D'Earley cried, pointing to the south-east where the movement, far from being an advance, or even a deployment inviting an encounter on the lower ground of their enemy's own choosing, was turning retrograde. D'Earley stood in his stirrups and looked along the

Royalist line, then sat back down again in his saddle, emitting his famous chuckle.

William, highly annoyed at the disobliging retreat of the enemy, could see no reason for mirth and said so.

'But my Lord, 'tis the banners on the baggage carts; they seem like more chivalry in our rear. They think us overwhelming.'

But William had no time for this, he was thinking hard, for it was now clear that FitzWalter was withdrawing into the lower town, the larger, southern portion of the city. He turned his horse and galloped back through the Royalist lines to regain height, drawing rein when he had a clear view of the castle, above which flew the banner of Nicola de la Haye.

The advance of the Royalist forces had begun to clear the Edge of any enemy forces of substance investing the west, and, or so it would seem, the north sides of the city.

'John,' he called to his nephew who, with D'Earley and the handful of knights forming William's personal body-guard, had followed him on his reconnaissance, 'take four men and see if you can get under the walls unmolested to send word to the Lady Nicola that we shall not abandon her.'

William watched for a moment as John Marshal rode off before returning to his place in the line of battle which stood, in bold array, frustrated of its carefully planned encounter. By the time he got back to the side of his son, Falkes de Bréauté, Ranulph of Chester, Longsword and Des Roches had all ridden in for orders.

'They have fooled us, God damn their souls,' snarled Ranulph of Chester.

'Not so,' William began, before being interrupted by Des Roches.

'But we have no siege engines, William.'

'The castle,' William said. 'I have sent John to reconnoitre. Do you take your crossbowmen forward. From what I have seen we might enter the castle, for its defences are much damaged. God knows how it has held out this long, and there is a large engine before it that we may use…'

There was a good deal of discussion, before Des Roches moved to obey William's order, whereupon there was a sudden disturbance among the commanders' escorts.

'My Lord!' They all turned to where a knight pointed out that: 'John Marshal is returning.' A few moments later William's nephew rode up with a strange knight beside him. Both men's horses were blown, suggesting a headlong flight.

John reined-in alongside William. 'This knight, my Lord,' explained John Marshal, indicating the stranger, 'is Geoffrey de Serland; he comes from the Lady Nicola directly and met me as I encountered four French knights, whom we beat off.'

De Serland came forward. 'My Lord Marshal, I give you greeting. The Lady Nicola saw your advance and begs you to come on with all your *bataille*. She can admit you into the castle and...'

'My Lord,' Longsword interjected, 'this is folly, to get ourselves caught within Lincoln spells disaster...'

'Aye,' added Ranulph. 'Better we draw off...'

William held up a placating hand. 'Let us not act hastily.' He turned to Des Roches. 'Do you my Lord Bishop, lead your men forward as I desired. Falkes shall support you. Clear the siege lines and when you are within bowshot of the castle walls, go forward with this fellow...' William turned to De Serland. 'If you got out, I presume you can get back in?'

'If we are lucky, my Lord, and number but two,' De Serland replied. 'There is a postern and the enemy have partially abandoned their western siege lines on your approach, though there are still men to the westwards of the city.'

'Then go, Peter, you have knowledge of the place. Pass through the castle postern and reassure the Lady Nicola and ascertain the true state of affairs regarding the enemy. In the meanwhile we must bring up the sumpter horses, feed the men and water their mounts.

***

The army stood to its arms after it had broken its fast. But such had been the early hour of its start that the day had not yet reached noon before the Bishop of Winchester rode back. De Serland came with him, with messages of thanks from Nicola de la Haye, but it was Des Roches' intelligence in which William was the more interested.

Realising the importance of his news, Des Roches was intent on milking it for all it was worth, claiming he knew what he had to reveal all along, but concealing what it actually was that he had discovered until William, driven almost to distraction, cut him short.

'Very well, my Lord Bishop, you have explained how the enemy now occupy the entire city, both its upper and lower parts, but what in the name of God is it that you hold from us for, I swear to you that if it proves mere bluster and we lose what we have gained...'

''Tis a blocked-up gate, My Lord,' said Des Roches with an oily triumph as the nobles surrounding him stirred uneasily. The spectre of division amongst his commanders rose again in William's imagination.

'And?'

'Its doing was ill-done and it leads directly into the city just exterior to the castle bailiwick...'

'From the west?' asked William anxiously.

'Aye, my Lord,' responded Des Roches in an insolent tone and feigning surprise, as if his explanation were not clear enough for even William's illiterate mind to grasp.

'If its doing is so ill-done,' asked William Longsword, 'how is it that our enemy has not yet exploited it? They have been here three long months...'

Des Roches shrugged, 'who knows, my Lord of Salisbury. What is not obvious from the inside, though discernible to a perceptive man, is even less so from the outer, but the mortar is weak and...'

'How long would it take to clear?' William broke in.

Des Roches shrugged. 'Two, mayhap three hours, if you employed sufficient men.'

'And in what state are the walls of the castle?'

'Much broken down by the enemy's mangonels and a *trébuchet*, there is a large *perrière* left before the postern...'

'And the city's walls?'

'In like state, though perhaps not so much so.'

William ignored the apparent contradiction in Des Roches's words and thought a moment before rapping out a series of orders. 'My Lord Bishop, your crossbowmen are to cover the ramparts.' Turning to Falkes de Bréauté he said, 'get your men forward to dig me out this gate, for by God I would go hence into the city by this route.'

'But my Lord…' began Ranulph of Chester before William stopped him short.

'You my Lord of Chester, shall have your desire and attack now, creating a diversion. Do you take your battalion around to the northern wall and see what might be achieved at the north gate. If you cannot break in, do whatever you may to draw off those within who might obstruct our path once we force this obstructed gateway…'

'If it exists,' Ranulph remarked sourly, glaring at Des Roches.

'Oh, it exists, my Lord of Chester,' Des Roches crowed, 'and the Lady Nicola will have her men cover us, that *I* have already arranged.' The man was positively preening himself.

'Did you also ask that the Bishop's Palace should be made ready for your arrival too?' asked Ranulph, to which Des Roches smirked, somewhat embarrassed. 'You did?' sneered the Earl, 'By the Rood, I hope your arms are as strong as your conceit!'

'My Lords!' William snapped. 'We have yet a hard day's work ahead of us. Now set aside our damnable jealousies. Salisbury, you shall hold the reserve.' William completed his dispositions and stared about him. 'Any questions? No? Very well, then to your posts, My Lords and Gentlemen, and may God go with you and may He crown our arms with victory and let us send the French and their English allies to Hell before the sun sets.' The chorus of 'Amens' was accompanied by breast crossing as the extemporised Council of War broke-up.

***

William eased himself behind a gorse or broom-bush; he was not sure which. He realised that he was taking an unnaturally long time in his evacuation, that he was muttering to himself, and that beyond the shelter of the gorse there was the sound of singing. The army were in high spirits, imbued with the cheerfulness of crusaders yet to be mauled by the enemy. He stared at the prickly bush in which he concealed his person and remembered Henry the Young King using it, the yellow *plante genet*, as his mesnie's token on one occasion at a tourney in the Vexin, but he could not recall where.

He felt queer; a sensation that was not the same as the nervous tension prior to action that he had experienced both in war and on the field of tournament. There was something wrong with him, something very wrong, that had begun with the frequent night-time pissing of which he had heard men who reached his age suffered. Now there was some malady in his bowels. He again recalled with dread the foul end of Curtmantle, a great King brought low by disease and a failing body. Was he, William Marshal, Earl of Pembroke and much else besides, destined for such a filthy and disgusting demise?

Still squatting over his excrement, he offered up a prayer. Better to die in battle than shitting in Isabelle's fine Irish linen, by God!

Suddenly resolute he rose and cleaned himself as best he could, then emerged from the bushes to where his squire waited with his coat of mail, surtout helm, sword and destrier.

A short distance off John D'Earley was mounting up at the head of a cluster of knights. Dragging on his coat of mail, William watched him take the Pembroke standard from a waiting squire and heft it. By the time William's head was clear of the surtout with its white cross, D'Earley was walking his horse towards him.

'The Bishop of Winchester reports the way is almost clear, my Lord. In my judgement, we should advance our power before the enemy knows what we are about.'

'Very well,' replied William, 'though I am sure that by now the enemy will have guessed.'

William mounted his destrier. It seemed the great beast could already scent the coming battle, for it stirred restlessly beneath him. He settled his sword and then kicked his charger forward.

'My Lord,' the squire reminded him, holding it out, 'your helm.'

'Eh?' William turned in his saddle. 'Not yet. I wish to see properly. Hold my lance too...'

Then he spurred the destrier to a canter as John D'Earley, his escort and his squires, fell in behind him.

***

The convenient gorse bush had been on the north face of Lincoln Edge and as William crested the low rise he saw the whole army astir. Away to the left – east wards – Ranulph's forces were already close to the old Roman gate in the north wall, while De Bréauté's were massing behind Des Roches' under the west wall, clustered around the enemy's abandoned *perrière,* exchanging a hail of arrows and cross-bow quarrels with the defenders, themselves under a shower of bolts from the walls of the castle.

Longsword's battalion was moving up and as William and his guard approached the city's west wall a horseman was observed riding pell-mell from the north-gate.

'My Lord!' the man cried as he drew rein in a swirl of dust, 'My Lord of Chester urges you to hasten! The north-gate is breached, for it had been left open for the remnants of the enemy retiring into the city and we forced it in their rear.

For a moment William considered diverting the entire attack, but as he waved Longsword forward another messenger arrived. Besides setting men to dig-out the filled-in west-gate, Falkes de Bréauté had taken half his men directly to the castle's small postern, which, being part of the city's western wall, opened onto the countryside. Shouting for it to be opened in the name of King Henry and the Marshal, he had stormed across the castle bailey taking with him some of Des Roches' cross-bowmen who, with his own archers, reinforced those defenders on the ramparts of the castle facing into the city, from where they redoubled the harrying of the enemy by the defenders.

'Even now, my Lord,' the messenger gasped breathlessly, 'he requests your support for the Lady Nicola refuses to open the east gate so that my Lord de Bréauté can debouch into the city!'

William looked about him. He could see the furious work being undertaken at the city's west-gate, but his eyes were rheumy and he asked D'Earley what he made of it.

'My judgement from here?' D'Earley asked.

'Aye.'

D'Earley screwed up his eyes. 'Perhaps we are almost through, perhaps not...'

'Christ's blood,' William snapped, 'hand over my standard, ride forward and find out!'

As D'Earley galloped off, William waved his son up beside him. 'Will, take your mesnie and go to Falkes' support. Use my authority to compel the Lady Nicola's men to yield and open the castle's east gate the moment I beak through this confounded obstruction.'

Once Will had gone, William waved the remainder of the army forward. 'Momentum,' he muttered to himself, 'we must maintain momentum and strike at as many points as we may.'

As he approached the city wall D'Earley rejoined him, accompanied by Peter des Roches. His eyes glittered through the slits in his helm. 'My Lord, we have men inside, they tear down the stones and bricks from both sides...'

'How long before we can pass a horse...?'

'A matter of minutes!'

'Then we advance...'

'My Lord, have a care,' Des Roches reached out and grabbed the bridle of William's destrier, 'we have yet to clear it properly, do not, I beg you attempt this thing piecemeal. Send forward scouts...'

'God's lance, Peter, the time for scouts is long past! John here tells me a horseman may pass and that is what we shall do,' he added, putting spurs to the destrier and calling over his shoulder for his squire to fetch his lance and helmet. 'Forward!' he roared.

'Be not hasty, my Lord!' cried Des Roches, 'If you are lost no matter that we gain the victory...'

But William had already couched his lance and his mesnie was on the move. D'Earley had grabbed the Pembroke banner from its temporary minder and the squire attending William was shouting, 'My Lord! My Lord! Your helm! Your helm!'

Seeing William determined to carry the gate the instant a single horseman could get through, Des Roches stood in his stirrups and bellowed at Longsword. 'Bring up your battalion, good my Lord!' Thereafter he fell-in behind William as the Earl checked his headlong advance and paused to lace his helmet.

As they approached the walls they crossed the enemy's abandoned siege lines, only to find they were not entirely empty. Passing the *perrière* a man emerged from beneath it. He must have been dozing, for he made directly for the assembled stone pile, as if eager to display his zeal to the approaching chivalry. Too late he realised his mistake; with a single cut of his sword, John Marshal sent the wretch's head bouncing ahead of them like a pig's bladder kicked by prentice boys.

By the time William and his immediate escort reached the west-gate it was almost cleared and could admit two horsemen at a time. As they rode up the men who had been labouring at this task jumped back, covered in lime dust, laughing and shouting to urge on the English chivalry as the column narrowed its front and followed William and D'Earley – who had lowered William's standard – through the opening. Behind William, Des Roches drew rein, blessed them with the sign of the cross and ordered them to take up their arms and follow their betters into the city. Then he urged forward the men under Longsword who were coming up behind.

'For God and the Marshal!' he bellowed. 'Here! God help the Marshal!'

***

By breaking into Lincoln through the north gate in the wake of the retreating besiegers, the Earl of Chester had attracted a counter-attack from the Anglo-French coming up from the lower town. But the gradient of the hill was sufficient to slow most of the enemy so that Ranulph had fought his way through the press of houses along the High Street to the point where it met the defunct Westgate Street before meeting serious resistance. And it was here that the column following William, Will Marshal, Des Roches, and William Longsword crashed into the enemy flank, beginning a furious *mêlèe*.

As William's men had debouched into Westgate Street, they received covering fire from the north rampart of the castle which rose upon their right. From here, and every other suitable vantage point of the entire circumvallation of the castle, the bowmen of Falkes de Bréauté and the Lady Nicola, took a deliberate aim at the struggling destriers of the French knights and their English allies as they struggled up the High Street from the south. As the fighting increased in intensity, the bowmen slipped out of the castle and occupied the houses lining the streets, from where they did dreadful execution, especially among the vulnerable horses. When De Bréauté finally sallied from the castle, he was quickly surrounded and captured, then as quickly retaken by his own men as William made his junction with Ranulph of Chester.

Seeing the mass of enemy horsemen and foot-soldiers in front of him, William drove his destrier at them at full tilt, aware that, with Des Roches encouraging the men at the breached gate, Longsword had forced his way forward to appear by his side.

Suddenly awake to the new enemy on their flank, a group of Anglo-French knights wheeled to their left, into Westgate Street, where William and Longsword met them in the shock of battle. Both recognised the device worn by the leading knight: that of Robert de Ropelai, whom William had last seen at Runnymead. De Ropelai drove at Longsword, shivering his lance before William, standing in his stirrups and wielding his sword, dealt a passing blow at his back that tumbled Ropelai from his charger.

The fight became fierce and bloody. No quarter was being called-for, nor any given. It was war *á outrance*, the niceties of the tourney cast aside in the battle for England itself. Confined by the narrow streets, the clash of arms, the shouts and exhortations, the whizz and *thunk* of quarrel and arrow, the neighs and screams of suffering horses and the shouts and shrieks of wounded men, seemed magnified as the tight swirl of killing moved slowly south.

Having long since flung his lance aside as useless in such tight circumstances, William laid about him with a fury that courted notice. The indecision and confinement of the enemy, unable to move reinforcements through the streets and under the vigour of the Loyalist assault, began to give ground. But it was slow going and hot work. The knights' destriers were unable to make much progress, rearing up and kicking forward with their steel-shod fore-hooves as they had been trained. William and Longsword fought side-by-side; John D'Earley, skilfully managing his charger with his knees, both advanced William's standard and covered his master's rear with his sword-arm as the two Earls pressed inexorably forward.

Eventually the furious *mêlèe* reached the west front of the cathedral where a long disused graveyard offered a space for the matter to be decided. Here, William realised, the fight began to ebb from the enemy. Those Anglo-French still coming up Lincoln's steep hill from their main encampment in the south were breathless by the time they reached this killing ground long occupied by death, and here – at the summit of the hill, outside the cathedral - William encountered Thomas, Comte de la Perche.

With Longsword and D'Earley close, and with De la Perche surrounded, William called upon his enemy to yield, reaching out to grab De la Perche's bridle.

'Never!' roaded De la Perche, causing his destrier to rear and tear the bridle from William's grasp.

'Yield my Lord Perche! For the Love of God, you can do no more here!' William bellowed above the din, but again De la Perche refused.

'God damn you, you French bastard!' roared a knight, coming up close with a shock, sword in hand.

'Croc!' shouted Longsword, who recognised Reginald Croc, one of Falkes de Bréauté's senior *routiers*, 'stay your hand!'

But it was too late. With considerable skill, De Croc thrust his sword through the *oiliére* of the French nobleman's helmet. Jerking backwards, his destrier again caracoling, De la Perche struck out with his own sword, held in both hands, hammering William with three tremendous blows upon his helm before toppling backwards over the rump of his destrier into the dust.

The fight had almost deserted the enemy and William was able to have one of his mesnie dismount and loosen De la Perche's helmet. When it was withdrawn the Count lay stone dead; Croc's dextrously placed *pointe* had penetrated De la Perche's brain.

William looked down upon the stricken Frenchman; the fact that they were distantly related did not then occur to him. That he had not been granted a death in battle and that its possible agent, De la Perche, had struck three great blows at him after being technically killed, did however.

With Longsword and William staring at the dead man, Croc sought to justify his action. 'The order was no quarter,' he spluttered.

'We have the upper hand,' riposted Longsword.

'You might have had ransom,' added Des Roches, riding up.

'The day is not yet ours,' snapped William, ending the diversion, and turning his attention back to the enemy on the lower slopes of Lincoln Hill with its narrow High Street.

While the death of De la Perche might have demoralised the French, there remained the forces of the English Barons under Quincy de Saur and Robert FitzWalter who, cast back down the hill, were reforming, urged on by the two chief rebel

Barons. However, they were in a weak position as the Loyalist forces came down the hill from the cathedral, their blood up and a decisive victory in prospect.

Slowly the rebels were forced back; then their resistance crumbled. First it was the foot-soldiers who, knowing that death or maiming awaited the defeated, abandoned their superiors. Then the knights, struggling against the press, their horses shot under them by crossbow-bolts, or hamstrung by the Royalist foot-soldiers, began to fall back, some on foot, to be seized as hostages. Finally the Barons and French magnates, bereft of support, increasingly exhausted and pressed downhill by the Loyalists, caved-in.

Then, just at the point at which William lifted his sword to order a general advance, Sir Alan Basset, whom William had left to guard the baggage train, appeared in the enemy's rear. Frustrated at being denied any part in the fight and unable to enter the city through the breached gate for the press of men still passing through, Basset had taken the initiative.

Descending the Edge and passing round the south-west corner of the city walls, Basset caught the flood of men pouring out of the southern gate, to cross the River Witham and escape southwards along Ermine Street.

The rebels emerging from the south gate found the lifting bridge an obstacle to their escape, for a wandering cow had blocked the mechanism which allowed the sponson to be raised and let barges through. Now the frightened and ensnared animal aided the Loyalists' cause. Some of the men trapped by this hapless creature jumped into the Witham, others sought escape, east and west, over the softer ground where, only that morning, they had lain in their siege lines, their main encampment a short distance off on the other side of the river. And behind them came the pursuing Loyalists, descending the hill pell-mell, Will Marshal in the van.

The younger Marshal burst through the gate, hacking left and right, his squire behind him bearing his own standard overshooting and falling – horse and all – into the river. Here, on the banks of the River Witham, the rebellious Barons of England made their last, feeble stand, and here at last Quincy de Saur and Robert FitzWalter fell into William's hands.

William drew rein alongside FitzWalter. 'Your sword,' he commanded abruptly, 'and unhelm.' Fitzwalter handed over his sword and removed his casque, whereupon William did the same. 'Where is Hugh of Arras?' he asked next, referring to the man who, under Louis' orders had, that Lenten-tide, laid siege to Lincoln and later summoned the help of others. FitzWalter shrugged.

'Escaped to the south, my Lord,' someone offered, 'with a handful of chivalry.'

Then Des Roches rode-up, his shield dented and his sword-blade bloody. 'The day is ours, my Lord Marshal,' he said gleefully, jostling his destrier close to William's. Then, removing his own helmet and leaning over his saddle-bow, he lowered his voice, 'Reginald Croc has been delivered to God's judgement.' William stared at Des Roches. Not for the first time the ambiguity of the man struck him. 'He killed De la Perche treacherously...' the Bishop explained.

'Upon your orders?' William asked.

'By mine own hand,' Des Roches replied.

'Fine work for a Christian Bishop,' William muttered, pulling his charger's head away from that of the Bishop's.

***

'Old habits die hard, eh, John?' William remarked with a grin, his hand about a large stoop of wine in the great hall of Lincoln Castle. John Marshal grinned back. Unlike their English allies, seeing their cause lost and no reason to fear their enemy's vengeance, many of the French knights had surrendered in the dying moments of the battle. Seizing the opportunity thus offered, some of the Loyalist knights had taken hostages in hope of ransom, John Marshal among them. 'What is your tally?'

'Seven, my Lord, all bannermen.'

221

'We have adequate accommodation for them, my Lord,' offered a delighted Lady Nicola, whose welcome of William and his principal men into the castle keep had been warm.

In the coming two days it became clear that he had dealt the enemy a telling blow: over three hundred knights and numerous sergeants-at-arms had fallen into the Royalists' hands. As for Lincoln, a heartless judgement being made by the Lord Bishop of Winchester that its citizens had given the enemy material support, the billeted army plundered the hapless townsfolk. Some terrified women and their children took to boats to escape the looting and rapine, only to drown when their over-loaded and inexpertly-handled vessels capsized.

Such local support of the rebels and, worst of all the French, was extended to the Church, whose clergy were thus excommunicated. As a consequence, Peter des Roches also led a ferocious assault on the cathedral treasury and encouraged the theft of everything ecclesiastical thereby most conveniently rendered 'unholy'. From his successor as Precentor, he looted eleven thousand marks in ingots of pure silver. It was indeed fine work for a Christian Bishop, and such was the jubilation among the victors, that they ever afterwards recalled the event as 'Lincoln Fair'.

But William took no part in these gross excesses. On the very evening of the battle, leaving Ranulph of Chester and William Longsword to prepare for a march on London, he and his close escort rode for Nottingham. Here William knelt before the young King who sat in state, the Papal Legate standing at his side, and laid the sword of FitzWalter at his feet.

'God has graced your arms, Sire. Lincoln is yours,' he said simply.

CHAPTER NINE - SANDWICH May – August 1217

William's body ached when he woke next morning. At the age of seventy-two he had spent twenty hours in the saddle the previous day and wielded his weapons with great energy for about three, but he had no hesitation in ordering the knights of his mesnie to ready themselves to ride out that Sunday morning.

It was the eve of the Feast of Pentecost and they rode out of Nottingham to the sound of chanting, a small piquet of four knights and eight sergeants-at-arms in the van, with John D'Earley bearing the great green and gold standard with its rampant read lion riding on William's quarter. D'Earley's arms ached too, but his heart burst with pride for again being the bearer of the Marshal's device. From time-to-time D'Earley regarded the man riding ahead of him for whom he felt he would lay down his life. The Marshal, as he was most popularly known, was the greatest man in the Kingdom, and it was not just John D'Earley who thought so.

D'Earley had been present the previous evening as William had presented FitzWalter's sword to the King. He had watched the young monarch, who had all the presence of an Angevin Prince which, D'Earley privately prayed, would not turn him into a man like his father, John, or his uncle, the Lionheart, or even his grandfather. Something better had to come out of this House of Anjou, something better for the Kingdom of England.

Without doubt, the boy possessed an innate intelligence and with it a precocity for which he was by now well-known. Nevertheless it had been rather a pathetic encounter, for nothing was yet certain in the future of Henry III. He might have been anointed King of England, but England was a divided realm and the lad's question to his Guardian expressed much of his personal anxiety.

Having bent to touch FitzWalter's sword as a gesture of acceptance, he had naively asked William, 'Have you secured me my Kingdom, my Lord Marshal?'

And Willian had responded, 'Not yet, Your Grace, though our work at Lincoln has dealt with a goodish part of your enemies. There yet remain those under the Dauphin in the south.'

'And how, my Lord, shall you deal with them? Pray tell me, for I am eager to understand the waging of war.'

'I pray, my Liege,' William had responded, 'that you never have to face a rebellion once this is over, but first I must let the dogs have their bones.'

'By which you mean..?'

'It is necessary, my Liege, to bind men to your cause by more than oaths of fealty. Few men risk their lives willingly for such notions, and honour and chivalry can be as shifting as sand. A great number of the enemy were taken at Lincoln…'

'You mean the rebel Barons?' the King had queried.

'Specifically, yes, though many common soldiers fell into our hands…'

'And what of them?'

'Many have been put to the sword, or otherwise disposed of.' Henry had nodded his satisfaction. 'But the Barons will be ransomed by their captors, and likely ruined thereby, though you may have the heads of FitzWalter and Quincy de Saur, or whomsoever else that pleases you should you wish it. The Comte de la Perche's was rolling down Lincoln High Street the last time I saw it,' William had said, with a grim smile and the King had laughed delightedly.

'So how long will you allow for this throwing of bones to my loyal dogs, for it would seem to me that a delay might prove fatal to our fortune. The Dauphin has only to obtain reinforcements from his father...' The King had broken off, non-plussed.

'Not long, Sire. I purpose to march south and arrange a great rendezvous at Chertsey, just south of the Thames, where I may cover the west and isolate the rebel garrisons in the west-country before striking east.'

'And London, my Lord, what of London, my capital and seat of my power? I would fain come thither.'

'Give me a little time, my Liege, and London will come to you.'

As they rode back toward Lincoln John D'Earley smiled to himself. He knew well that few of the rebel Barons had actually died at Lincoln. William, with Longsword, had already laid a claim to the domains of the dead Comte de la Perche, citing their tenuous relationship with the man. As for the others, the survivors, their lands would now be forfeit and he, D'Earley could expect to profit by grants of manors and markets now in William's gift.

FitzWalter had pleaded for clemency, claiming that, although one of the Council of Twenty-five, his hatred of King John had been engendered by the late King's seduction of his daughter Matilda. Declaring he intended to go on crusade to the Holy Land would doubtless secure him his life, D'Earley mused, for William was not an overly vindictive man and was capable of a certain disingenuity where matters of state were concerned, whatever words he used to the young King. Besides, the Papal Legate would probably permit such an act of contrition on FitzWalter's part.

***

In prospect of great rewards and riches himself, William had answered the Loyalist Barons' expectations and thrown the dogs their bones, arranging Chertsey as the place of rendezvous after they had secured their prisoners and made known the conditions for their ransom and release. Ranulph of Chester rode off to Mountsorrel to raze that pestilential fortress to the ground while John Marshal gleefully dealt with his seven hostages, to his great advantage.

For his own part William called Thomas to his side and dictated a long letter to Isabelle, detailing the outcome, for the brief cessation of hostilities was as much for William's benefit as his Loyalist 'dogs'.

With Longsword, William carved up De la Perche's English lands, including Royal Manors which the Comte's family had held at the Royal pleasure. Ironically, William secured Newbury, where, more than half a century earlier, he had been a child-hostage of King Stephen. As for his mesnie, all received rewards consistent with their rank and service, further cementing their loyalty to his person.

These arrangements being either concluded or well set in train, William ordered the army to march south. Besides his preoccupations with securing as much advantage from his victory as he could, William had not entirely neglected the business of war. By the time he left Lincoln he knew that Louis had returned to batter the ramparts of Dover Castle with his massive *trébuchet*, and that the Cinque Port men were active in the Strait intercepting the reinforcements sent by Philippe to his son's aid.

As the Loyalist army moved south they came across evidence of the fate of those who had escaped Lincoln, for in their desperation the Anglo-French fugitives had sought sustenance from the towns and villages through which they fled. What they received was death and mutilation, a payment for their own northwards advance of rapine and plunder, so that fewer than ten score reached London with news of the disaster at Lincoln.

When the news of the battle reached Louis on the 25th May the Dauphin had raised the siege of Dover and retired to London, arriving on 1 June. Five days later William encamped at Chertsey where he was not only rejoined by the Barons and knights who had fought at Lincoln, but by others who, seeing the way the wind blew and disaffected by the French attitude towards the English, were deserting the Anglo-French cause in increasing numbers.

Regarding several of these defectors, D'Earley heard William growl to himself: 'So now we have a better prospect: to fight the French alone...'

This was to prove something of a simplification, but D'Earley grasped the Marshal's strategic vision, for it was clear that the Dauphin's position was one of growing isolation. Word filtered across the Strait of Dover that King Philippe was preoccupied with having the Papal Interdiction against him and his son's cause lifted, so-much-so that he had grievously neglected the matter of reinforcing Louis. This task had been taken up by the Dauphin's wife, Blanche of Castile, though in truth it yielded little. The English seemed to be masters of the Strait and there was little money to raise troops and none to pay the French seamen who might be induced to convey them to Sandwich or London.

However, within a week of quartering his army along the banks of the Thames, William received a delegation of churchmen, abbots chiefly, but led by the Archbishop of Tyre. Meanwhile, London was in ferment, its citizens havering between declaring for Henry and ejecting Louis, or standing by the French Prince to whom they had collectively declared their loyalty. That they did not abandon the invaders, who were far from welcome, rested entirely on two factors, the presence among them of an armed force of occupation and the fate of Lincoln's citizens.

These circumstances led to a stalemate which in turn resulted in a change of fortune and a dispersal of the Loyalist forces. Although many had come into the Loyalists' camp, most of the great magnates unaffected by Lincoln, aware of what might happen to them should they find themselves the objects of Royal vengeance, remained loyal to Louis. There were some exceptions, among them the Earl de Warenne.

Ever mindful of the limits of the Royal Treasury, William, unable to pay the growing army and perceiving all his gains at Lincoln to be in jeopardy, allowed it to disperse, retiring himself to Oxford, whither came the King and Guala di Bicchieri. He was greatly influenced by a stirring in the west, where the Welsh Princes under Llewelyn had again raided as far south as the Gower and besieged William's own castle at Haverfordwest.

Once more he climbed into the saddle and made a sweep to Chepstow and Goodrich, but could spare neither time not thought for a proper raid deeper into the disputed territory. The young King's plea on leaving Oxford rang in his ears: 'My Lord Marshal, you promised me my Kingdom...'

That both sides were now almost equally weakened was cold consolation; there seemed to William no way of executing a fatal wound upon Louis. Lincoln had taught him in fact what he already knew, that desultory war, sieges and exchanges of castles, essentially altered nothing. He had ordered the revised *Magna Carta* promulgated throughout the land, including all those parts that had, after Lincoln, fallen under the notional government of Henry, and this had had some effect upon those who had arrived at Chertsey, but such a *demarché* did not constitute anything more than a statement of intent. Without routing Louis and the rebel Barons, war would sputter on and on, and William was growing old and tired of it.

He found Chepstow bleak without Isabelle, for by mutual consent she and the younger children had withdrawn to Leinster where, whatever befell England, she remained an Irish Princess.

But it was at Chepstow, on the eve of his return to the King's side at Oxford, that he conceived the strategy by which he might – just might – finally turn the tables on Philippe Augustus's plan to establish his son on the throne of England, and it was John D'Earley, loyal, grinning John, who among all of William's considerable and noble following unwittingly put the notion into William's head.

They sat late at board, unwilling, it seemed, to return to the world of English politics. True, the *chevauchée* into the Welsh March had been limited and unsatisfactory, settling nothing more than showing some menace to the Welsh, but it *had* smacked of the old days. As is the way of such things it had revived memories of what now seemed a happier, more carefree time, when the Marshal and his mesnie, in all their vigour, had campaigned west, through Carmarthen, 'in the pouring bloody rain,' someone reminded them all. The reminiscence failed to dull the glitter of the memory.

Over their wine the senior knights of William's mesnie grew loud in their recollections, dwelling chiefly on the mishaps that had occurred, but had passed off well in the end. D'Earley had jested that when William had crossed over into Ireland to lay claim to the hand of the Lady Isabelle the ship had been so rotten that a portion of the deck had given way, causing the Marshal to fall and gash his leg. William's torrent of oaths had shocked even the Master of the vessel, who had wrung his hands with apologies and claimed he knew nothing of the state of the deck-timbers when William threatened to hang him.

This had led to several other anecdotes of the vagaries of sea passages and while his companions roared with laughter over stories of vomiting, falling over, breaking arms and banging heads, followed by more serious and tragic recollections of fine destriers breaking their legs in the holds of ships working in heavy seas, William was uncomfortably reminded of the last news from the Cinque Ports to reach him at Oxford. That the English vessels had fought a series of actions against the French had seemed to him at the time but a providential interruption of the efforts of Blanche of Castile to assist her husband. Now, however, something struck him and he rose suddenly from his seat and, head-down and ignoring all those at board, he began pacing the chamber. Gradually, one-by-one, the half-drunk company fell silent, watching and waiting, like unmasked hawks.

After some moments William stopped pacing and turned to the expectant faces of his trusted companions. With collective relief they saw that he was smiling.

'I cannot think why I have not seen this before,' he said in a low voice, 'but surely the method of war we should now pursue is not one on land, but on the sea...'

A murmur of interest rose among the men in the great hall of Chepstow as they looked at each other and waited for what was coming.

'Formerly,' William said with mounting enthusiasm, 'we have besieged castles, exchanged territory as the sway of fortune allowed. At sea war is different, for it is just advantage that sways this way and that. First we lost ground because the men of the Cinque Ports defected to the rebels, then, when they regained their senses, our cause prospered awhile. Louis' luck during his long and imperfect siege of De Burgh at Dover rose and fell according to the presence of French or English ships of war lying off that place and now, as we have so recently learned, such reinforcements as Blanche of Castile would throw across the water may be compromised by lack of ships, or seamen, or money, or all three together, but can most certainly be stopped by English vessels.

'My Lords and Gentlemen, Louis needs command of the Strait to accomplish *anything*. He has the Thames, true, but the Thames lies beyond the Strait. The Strait, it seems to me, is a battle-ground we have not yet fully exploited, for it is Louis' weak-point, not ours.

'Is it not therefore politic that we should invest our hopes in our ships and mariners, who may carry our chivalry to dispute this place to our advantage?'

William looked round at the upturned faces. 'Come, my Lords and Gentlemen, what do you say?'

'These are not circumstances we well understand, my Lord,' said the younger Marshal. 'The enemy have Eustace the Monk to direct their fleet, and all men know that black demon of a man knows more of the sea than any man alive…'

'More than the mariners of the Cinque Ports?' riposted William. 'I daresay he knows as much, and that noble blood flows in his veins, but I will wager that we may find men among the mariners of Dover and Winchelsea and Rye and the other places who, should we repose our confidence in them, may bring our cause to its desired haven.'

'I my Lord, I think you are right,' said Philip d'Aubigny decisively.

'So do I,' added John Marshal.

These forceful endorsements entirely overset young Will's misgivings and, in the uproar of enthusiasm that followed, William called for quiet.

'Very well. We shall ride to Oxford tomorrow as planned and send out orders for a muster – of both men and ships.'

***

'My Liege, with your permission, I would appoint Philip d'Aubigny and my nephew John Marshal the chief captains of this most Royal muster of your ships.'

'Think you this will fare better than the muster at Chertsey, my Lord Marshal?' squeaked the King acidly.

'Nothing is more certain in war than that it is an uncertain business, Sire,' William replied. 'It demands constant shifts and changes; what seemed possible in the morning may be ruined by a torrent of rain in the afternoon. I think only that it

236

offers a chance, no, more than a chance. But we should have embraced such a strategy earlier, notwithstanding that it costs a great deal of money. However, if you will give to the mariners some inducement such as is enjoyed by knights in the field...'

'But they are commoners, villeins, my Lord; no, no, such a thing is not possible...'

'They are masters of their craft, my Liege,' William explained patiently. 'Just as Your Grace, out of a prospect of good governance yielded certain concessions in the *Magna Carta* but lately issued in your name, you will purchase some regard by so doing.'

The young man frowned uneasily and William perceived signs of his heritage; here was a John unwilling to shift his thinking for fear of the consequences. And then a thought occurred to him.

'You may buy men's love, Sire, very easily by such acts. Your noble father gained much among these men by his going amongst them in his hour of need.'

The young man looked up. 'He did?'

'Indeed he did.'

'Then why did they turn against him?'

'Because, my Liege, he was inconstant. Great men cannot afford to be inconstant. It was something your father never learned.'

Henry looked sharply at William. 'Is not that *lésé majesté*, my Lord?'

'Not if it is the truth.'

'You rebuke me, my Lord.'

'I seek to instruct you, Sire,' William responded firmly. 'It is my privilege.'

***

William had not sought the King's commission for his nephew and Philip d'Aubigny simply because they had been the first to endorse his maritime strategy, for he had offered command first to Peter des Roches, Bishop of Winchester. Des Roches was still smarting from wrongs, real and imagined, he perceived done to him during the attack on Lincoln, arguing that William had exceeded his authority and treated his advice with contempt, that William's profits from the battle exceeded his own, notwithstanding that acquisition of the Preceptor's silver marks. Unwilling to make an enemy of Des Roches, William had sought to restore good relations, but upon being offered this opportunity, De Roches had scoffed.

'I am no seaman, nor a pirate, nor a fisherman,' he retorted, adding by way of Parthian shot, 'go yourself and die!'

With a sigh of disappointment William had turned upon his heel, the breach between them fatal.

With the King in his train, William left Oxford at the head of a considerable military following and headed first for Reading. By mid-August he was at Farnham Castle, returned to Royalist hands. From here he rode on to Lewes, from where he sent Henry to Canterbury. William reached the coast at Romney on the 19th.

All along the road William had been greeted by townsfolk who regarded him as a conqueror, a circumstance which greatly embarrassed him, and this sense of inadequacy increased once he arrived within sight of the Channel, sparkling in the August sunshine. Summoning the chief men of the Cinque Ports to a colloquy he learned that morale amongst them was low. Despite the arguments he had made in their favour to the King, many still resented the impositions of King John and, worse still, they had in the preceding few days received a severe defeat by the French in an action off Calais in which many had abandoned their vessels under full sail and escaped in their ships' shallops. It did not augur well, but William urged that every sea-captain and mariner of worth and note be called to hear what he had to say and, two days later he addressed upwards of a hundred of these grizzled, wind-blown men.

In his many crossings of both the English Channel and St George's Channel, to say nothing of his voyage to the Holy Land, William had made the acquaintance of many seafarers, both mariners and common seamen. Most were, like himself, unlettered, but he had learned that among the mariners, those who commanded and directed the movements of ships, there were those who possessed a vast body of knowledge relating to tides, the presence of sandbanks and shoals and the predicting of the weather. That they were not infrequently overwhelmed and lost their lives was a testament not to their incompetence, but to their environment and its uncertainties. As to their weaknesses, they were common enough: drink and women, and, of course money. But then what man was not moved by these several springs? The only difference between the Cinque Port men and other seafarers was, William knew, they regarded themselves as England's prime mariners, men whose ancient role had been debased and under appreciated by John.

Armed with such insights and flanked by Philip d'Aubigny and John Marshal, he rose to speak. It was instantly clear that the presence of so great a magnate among them as William Marshal commanded something like respect.

'I will not trouble you with any courtly preamble, good-men all, but I come in the King's name to make you an offer upon which you have my own word, that to you shall be restored to you all your privileges and franchises taken from you by our late King, and that without asking anything further of you. I know you to be high in the King's regard, and in my own, as being the chief mariners in the Kingdom.

'But I know too, that you have been but recently humbled by the French and I am told to your shame, that some among your company did abandon their ships, affrighted by the enemy. I cannot think that any mariner of England sleeps comfortably with that infamy despoiling his honour, honour and valour having been previously shown by you against the enemy. What I lay before you is the prospect of restoring that honour and of adding to its glories in the service you are enjoined by ancient statute and charter to render unto the King's Grace.

'Moreover, such dutiful obedience unto the task I shall set before you will earn you all the blessings of the church, that we may take back this Kingdom which is rightfully that of our Sovereign Prince, King Henry, third of that name, and, under his good government, ours to prosper in.

'What good do you think shall come out of rule by Louis and vassalage to the King of France? Where then your ancient

241

privileges, your pride, your independence? You have triumphed before and shall triumph again. What occurred off Calais was a chastening by God, a humbling and the time is now upon you to embrace your true task, to keep the Channel for England. Think on these things and give me your answer in one hour…'

With that William and his two companions withdrew. It took a mere twenty minutes for the short hubbub of argument that followed William's departure to die-down. He learned afterwards that it had been suggested that whether or not the Marshal's proposition was to be accepted, the restoration of their privileges carried the day; the matter was not even put to any vote, as was customary among them. A request came for William, John Marshal and D'Aubigny to return to the Moot Hall in which the meeting had been convened.

'We will willingly and right gladly hear what you require of us, my Lord Marshal, a spokesman said, and for a second time William stepped forward.

'Good-fellows all, I would have you place yourselves under the command of these Lords who accompany me, My Lord D'Aubigny and John Marshal, of mine own kin. I would have you also prepare and muster as many men of good heart and spirit that you may and bring them to the place of rendezvous which I leave unto you…'

'Sandwich, my Lord,' someone shouted. The assertion was followed by cries of 'Aye, Sandwich,' and it was as if they all divined what William now set before them.

'Very well. Sandwich it is, and from there you shall, at a moment favourable to you as regards the wind and tide and of your own choosing, carry forces under the King's standard, against the French. Whatever you desire in your hearts regarding reward, ransoms and advantages, hear this: it is my desire that you utterly rout the enemy and to that end my Lord D'Aubigny, with other men of rank and following, will embark with you. I therefore charge that you shall, with all your might and main, press upon the enemy even unto the gates of Calais, until you have achieved the saving of England.

'Will you do it? What say you..?'

The second question was drowned in cheering and William left the Moot Hall with the remark that 'if enthusiasm could be harnessed and sprung like a mangonel, Louis was already lying in the dust.'

***

William returned to Canterbury to find the new Justiciar of England, Richard de Chilham, disputing the command of the forces then mustering at Sandwich and making a case for his own candidacy before the King. De Chilham, a bastard son of King John by Earl Warenne's sister, was backed up by De

Warenne, who, having given up the rebel side, had thrown his lot in with the King and now wished for his family to cover itself in glory. Henry looked to William for advice.

'My Liege,' William said wearily, 'if my Lord Justiciar wishes to venture his life afloat he is most welcome. The outcome of a sea-battle is unlikely to rely so heavily upon a single command as one on land and I am sure that Lord D'Aubigny's sensibilities may be flattered into submission. Besides, mayhap an edge of rivalry between two divisions of a fleet would work to advantage...' He was too tired to say more, and felt his sickness stirring within him.

Early next morning, shortly before sunrise, William led a cavalcade out of Canterbury to follow the road that ran along the line of the River Stour which debouched into the sea through the thriving port of Sandwich. Among the company rode D'Aubigny, De Chilham, De Warenne, John and Will Marshal. D'Aubigny had not demurred at the suggestion of divided command. Unfamiliar with naval warfare he saw in the pushy presence of the Justiciar a scapegoat if things went awry. As for William's nephew, John Marshal, his appointment was to the land forces which would garrison Sandwich as its menfolk almost to a man – and boy – went aboard the twenty or so hurriedly prepared vessels, along with a great number of knights, sergeants-at-arms and archers.

William bore the ride badly, reminded of Henry Curtmantle's failure to remain in the saddle during the last weeks of his fatal illness. From time-to-time he felt a pain like a dagger thrust into his bowel, but he stayed on horseback after they had arrived in the sea-port, where news had arrived from the cliffs of the Isle of Thanet to the north, that a French fleet was at sea.

Walking his horse up and down the quay as he watched the men go aboard he watched the ship-men at their unfamiliar work.

'What is in those?' he asked some men as they rolled barrels towards the gang-plank of a large vessel. William feared it was strong beer and while he was not insensible of the advantages of men fighting whilst drunk, he was not keen to encourage it.

''Tis slaked-lime, my Lord,' came the answer. 'We throw it in the vizzards of the French,' he added with a broad grin.

'Happen they be to looard,' his companion added.

'Oh, aye, happen they be well to looard!'

Nodding his satisfaction William stood in his stirrups and roared out encouragement: 'Go with God, good-fellows all, your cause is just and you should have the better hand in the game than your enemy, for know you that God has delivered him into your hands and he awaits you even now in the middle of the sea…'

In the middle of this exhortation Hubert de Burgh arrived from Dover, begging a command, citing his long and determined defence of Dover and his position as Justiciar of England under John.

'We might as well have one Justiciar more or less,' remarked William, knowing that none of the nobles embarked would achieve any glory that day without the co-operation and skill of the mariners. Once the fleets were in action it mattered little what a man's station in life was. The only difference was that, if captured, the nobles would be ransomed, the commoners tossed overboard, or worse.

Once the fleet had sailed, driving their ships downstream with any amount of noise, warping and poling, for they were grossly over-crowded and needed some offing before setting sail properly, William sought a place to rest, to await the outcome and – above all – to pray.

All that day a preternatural peace lay over the Kentish port. It was the Feast of St Bartholomew, the 24th August, a warm enervating day on shore. The wind came and went, fitful and fickle. William lay in an upper chamber of an inn near the waterfront, his body-servant and Thomas idling outside, swatting flies and chaffing the serving women in an attempt to pass the hours congenially.

The first news they had boded ill. It had been no coincidence that the French had appeared that morning. Fishermen arrived at the town quay to land their catch and told of a great fleet that had left Calais to disembark reinforcements sent to Louis by Blanche of Castile. It was purely circumstantial that the English war-fleet had been preparing for battle and the French arrival was merely convenient. What was less so, was the news that military reinforcements meant the enemy was well equipped to contest their passage.

John Marshal stood his men to arms, in case the enemy appeared in the Wensum Channel and entered the Stour, but the hours passed and no enemy appeared. Only the clear weather of the morning vanished. Instead a haze and then a mist limited the visibility, so that no watcher on the cliffs of Thanet could see anything beyond a mile or so to seaward.

The day drew on and towards sunset another fishing boat arrived. Aboard were two French knights from whom little could be learned beyond the fact that a great fight had taken place that day and, by all accounts, Eustace the Monk had been slain. Preoccupied by pain, William retired early with orders to be woken if any further intelligence came in.

It was not until the following day that anything positive was known. An English nef sailed up the Stour with news of a complete victory. Thereafter the returning English vessels came upstream in ones and twos bearing hostages and a rich plunder. All William truly understood of the sea-fight was that after some preliminary manoeuvring, during which it appeared the French formed the impression that they had, once again, bettered their opponents, Hugh de Burgh had turned his vessel about and led the attack from the rear. As the English fleet bore-up, the action fast became the general *mêlée* William had predicted. Eustace's flagship, which was overloaded with destriers and arms and bore treasure for the Dauphin, had been taken, Eustace had been cornered cowering in the hold and killed by a Cinque Ports master-mariner even as his flagship sank under him. As the action had become general the French vessels had, one-by-one, been overwhelmed, sinking or surrendering and yielding up a considerable booty. The enemy had been thrown into the sea, seamen and common soldiery alike, or put to death, so that of the puissant fleet that had sailed from Calais, only three dozen noblemen were landed at Sandwich.

When, that evening D'Aubigny came to William to formally report the outcome, William fell on his knees. '*Deo Gratias,*' he murmured, crossing himself. 'England is saved.'

CHAPTER TEN - CAVERSHAM - 1217 - 1219

William had been constantly active since the spring of that year and even after the Battle of Sandwich his labours were far from over. Louis received news of the disaster to his fleet on Saturday 26th August and agreed to meet William and De Burgh on Blackheath under flags of truce. Louis manoeuvred for time, arguing that he had agreed to meet Henry's envoys under duress. Further talks were necessary. London remained loyal to the Dauphin and, in his own opinion, Louis blustered that he was not yet beaten.

On De Burgh's advice, William had ordered the Cinque Ports ships round the North Foreland to blockade the Thames and cut off London from any supply by sea.

The action angered many of the Loyalist Barons who considered that, upon its fall, London should be subjected to the rapine and looting accorded to all cities that had supported an enemy. But, given the parlous state of the King's Exchequer and Treasury, William opposed this folly, declaring the needs of the Crown and the Kingdom came before any rewards to individuals, notwithstanding the honour gained by the claimants. It was clear from these dissensions that the French must be ejected from the Kingdom without further delay.

Among the French barons in London a creeping realisation that the game was up led them to plan a grand sortie, intended to permit their escape. They had for months been launching *chevauchée* after *chevauchée* into the country around London. But William, in a letter written by the faithful Thomas, proposed a meeting on an ait in the Thames, west of London. William, Longsword, Warenne and Arundel would guarantee Louis' safety.

It was two days before the Treaty of Kingston was agreed; William's terms were nevertheless generous. Louis was to leave England with all his power and chivalry, promising never to return. All castles in his hands were to be given up, as were those held in his name by the Welsh and Scots. By agreement with Guala di Bicchieri, all those rebels English hitherto excommunicated were restored to the love and charity of Holy Church and they would also enjoy all the privileges and liberties, the rights and advantages granted in the second *Magna Carta* issued under the great seal of Henry, the unequivocal King of England and third of that name. Most conciliatory of all was the provision that the surviving rebel

Barons would have all lands they possessed *ante bellum* restored to them. It amounted to a general amnesty.

Many considered the conditions to which William – in Henry's name – put his seal, far too lenient, especially his grant to Louis of an indemnity of fifteen thousand marks, but for English Barons like himself holding lands in Normandy, the inducement was essential and the raids of the French knights out of London had to be stopped before the damage they caused became excessive.

'It buries enmity,' William growled at his critics, chief among them Peter des Roches, who refused to pay the tax necessary to raise the money to indemnify Louis. In the end, only a fraction of it was ever handed over. Apart from the restoration of their domains to the rebellious Barons, the most unpleasant impact of the treaty on English soil was Louis' abandonment of the clergy who had clung to his cause. The Papal Legate insisted he be allowed to deal with them.

Guala di Bicchieri was kinder to the French enemy. He absolved the departing French troops, though they were to do penance, marching to Dover in bare feet and their breech-clouts, though Louis was allowed his surtout. Here the French took ship for France and on 29 October, a year almost to the day, the young King Henry rode into his capital to the acclamation of its fickle citizens.

Far to the north Ranulph, Earl of Chester, with the Earl of Derby alongside him, having ravaged Mountsorrel, raided deep into the countryside, taking castles and ejecting their castellans as the rebel cause foundered. On 19 December an accord was reached with King Alexander of Scotland who had held onto Carlisle but was also hereditary Earl of Huntingdon. Under an escort Alexander met the young Henry at Northampton and swore fealty for his English earldom.

As Christmas approached an uneasy peace settled over England and William and King Henry celebrated the Holy Festival of the Nativity at Gloucester.

***

Hardly had he laid aside the sword but William must take up the administration of the Kingdom. Its condition was parlous. There was no money in the Treasury, the disbanded soldiery were short of pay, the now unemployed knights demanded to resurrect the tourney to support themselves, the Court of King's Bench had not sat for nine years and the economy was stagnant. Worst of all, from William's perspective, was the clash of personalities consequent upon the terms of the Treaty of Kingston and the minority government of the King. Despite ravaging the northern Baronies, seat of the civil war just ended, the Earls of Chester and Derby, joined by the unreliable Aumale, refused to ratify it with their seals. Ranulph of Chester, so narrowly missing the role of Guardian, now laid joint claim to it, reforming a loose and dissenting confederation of the northern Barons, while Hubert de Burgh, the castellan of Dover, and Peter des Roches, Bishop of Winchester, formed an opposition to William nearer to home.

In failing health, William struggled on. He summoned a Great Council at Westminster that October, chiefly to raise money to pay Louis' indemnity by a scutage of two marks per knight, but also to ban the tournament. Falkes de Bréauté joined Des Roches in refusing to pay and William pledged revenues from his own lands to go some way to meet some of the obligation undertaken at Kingston. Orders went out to the judiciary to re-establish the Exchequer and, in January, William himself attracted an insolent disdain from Des Roches for sitting at the chequered cloth. His illiteracy was held by the Bishop to mark him both innumerate and a fool.

But William was far from either; he possessed the shrewdness of many an ill-educated man, sharpened by the knowledge of his own approaching death. Amid the turmoil of land-grabs, he acquired what he conceived to be his due and would be necessary to support his family, but unlike others he sought to rebuild a Kingdom which could sustain these ambitions as much for the Marshal inheritance as for the

House of Anjou. And when, shortly after Christmas 1217, the two coincided, he went again to war.

Under the terms of the Treaty of Kingston those Welsh Princes who had acted in loose alliance with the Dauphin were obliged to swear fealty to Henry III. Llewelyn bowed the knee, but Morgan ap Howell refused. Nursing an old grievance, Morgan captured the castle of Caerleon-upon-Usk taken from his family years earlier by the Lady Isabelle's father, Richard Strongbow, declaring that as long as William Marshal held an inch of Welsh soil in the name of Henry of Anjou, he would fight.

William despatched John D'Earley at the head of a substantial force which included the younger Marshal to recover the castle, but Morgan met D'Earley, and in the savage fighting that ensued, D'Earley's men were mauled, reducing matters to a stalemate. In March 1218 William called a grand parley at Worcester. In the King's presence, Prince Llewelyn laid down a plea that Caerleon be returned to Morgan ap Howell and he was supported by Peter des Roches and Ranulph of Chester.

'Men are never satisfied, but that they must endlessly carp and criticise,' grumbled William on the evening that Des Roches and Ranulph had spoken out. He was in pain and, in the absence of Isabelle, from whom he had concealed his chronic disability, he sought consolation in the company of the most faithful of his men.

'Both Chester and my Lord Bishop are in open opposition to you, my Lord,' said D'Earley, stung by his defeat at the hands of Morgan ap Howell and angry on William's behalf at the effrontery of the two men.

'They are not the only ones,' William remarked. 'The question is, what is to be done about it, for I must return a reply on the morrow?'

'What is in your Lordship's mind?' D'Earley asked.

'My mind is inclined to conciliation...'

'No father!' snapped his son, 'Morgan defiled and burnt a score of churches and laid waste the land, we lost ten of your best knights and he has been excommunicated. You cannot yield Caerleon to such a barbarian!'

William smiled ruefully. 'Morgan ap Hywell is no barbarian, Will,' he admonished gently. 'Do not forget you spring from your mother's womb as much as my loins and she is commonly regarded as a barbarian by the savages from the Brabant and France whom we so lately vanquished.'

Stung, Will flushed and responded with a grave formality. 'Very well, my Lord, then my advice is put it to the test of combat and I shall stand champion in your name. I have heard you offered such a solution to matters touching your own honour.'

The day following John D'Earley spoke for William's party, arguing that Morgan ap Howell was a rebel, allowing Henry to turn to William for advice. In the presence of the opposition of Ranulph and Des Roches, William's response was masterly.

'The fate of Caerleon lies in your gift, Sire. It was mine and was taken unlawfully in this time of peace by a rebel Prince, but it is no longer mine since it is in the hands of another and being so, is not in your hands either. The noble Prince Llewelyn, here present in good faith and being in love and good grace with yourself, my Liege, being linked with your house through marriage, would prove a most excellent castellan of Ceredigion and Carmarthen and, as Lord of Gwynedd and being in amity with myself as being Lord of the Southern March, would preserve Your Grace's peace throughout your Kingdom. This, I submit to you, Sire.'

Henry could only judge in William's favour. Caerleon was returned to him and an aggrandised Llewelyn must tell Morgan to evacuate the place and then make his peace with Ap Howell.

'By Christ's bones did you see the look upon the faces of Chester and Winchester,' guffawed D'Earley later, his good humour quite restored after William's brilliant discomfiture of the Prelate and the Lord of the Northern March. 'Even now they will be gnawing upon their own bowels, God rot them.'

William's conciliation, though not completely subduing the ambitions of the Welsh Princes, nevertheless led to a great oath-taking by many of them at Worcester in late May. It was as much as he could hope for and as much as he could achieve, for he had greater problems in England. The restoration of all lands to their Lords as held before the rupture of civil war had left most castles in the hands of John's appointees and although they had taken opposing sides in the rebellion, one characteristic marked their conduct: they were united in their rapacity. Contemptuous of a boy-king and a septuagenarian regent, they reverted to the plundering of the countryside and it was clear to William that while his failing physical condition precluded him from taking the field against them all, he should make an example of one or two. The question was – which? The matter was settled by the Bishop of Lincoln.

'My Lord Bishop complains that Newark Castle has not been returned to him as it should have been, my Lord,' Thomas reported one day, indicating the missive that lay before him as the two men sat in a chamber of The Tower of London. 'He sends one hundred marks against expenses, and requests that you restore the place to him, with its revenues.'

257

'Newark, eh?'

'Aye, my Lord.'

Both men were thinking the same thing. Newark was where John had died and it had therefore a symbolic significance to the power of young Henry. It had been in the fiefdom of the Bishop of Lincoln, but was being held by Robert de Gaugy in defiance of the terms of the Treaty of Kingston. William sighed, then smote the board before him and let out an imprecation.

'May such disloyal bastards be thrown into Hell without redemption! Write Thomas! Summon my nephew John and his mesnie, and tell the mayor and burgesses of Stamford that I require the services of thirty good miners to muster there by late July...say the 23rd or 24th. And order siege engines advance towards Newark at once. Send Will as escort...'

With King Henry at his side, on 8 July 1218, William Marshal, Earl of Pembroke, Lord of Leinster and Guardian of the Realm of England led a substantial force north out of London. He did not know it for sure, but he felt in his bones that he was going to war for the last time.

Besides his own and John Marshal's mesnie, William also commanded the Bishop of Lincoln's knights who joined him at Stamford. It was among these that the main casualties were caused as they charged into Newark and seized the town to prevent De Gaugy's men burning the towns-peoples' dwellings and thereby depriving the besiegers of cover from which to conduct operations. After a few days' hiatus as Will Marshal brought the slow-travelling siege engines up and placed them about the castle, which abutted the River Trent on one side.

But now William was personally obliged to withdraw to Nottingham, whence he had sent the King for safety, but where he shortly afterwards followed for fear of betraying the pain he was in. Will and John Marshal were left to begin siege operations. Happily these did not last long. The very appearance of the grim visaged old man at the head of a determined force had changed De Gaugy's mind and a surrender was negotiated.

William and Henry returned to London. There was little more William could do, though in November he ensured that the proceedings of the Court of King's Bench were revived. All around him his younger associates of so many crucial years were falling away, some, like Des Roches and Ranulph, in opposition; others, like the Papal Legate Guala de Bicchieri 'from exhaustion'. That December Pope Honorius III sent Cardinal Pandolpho back to England.

William spent Christmas at Marlborough, near the scenes of his childhood, dreaming in the winter sunshine in the company of Isabelle.

'Where are my chicks, Belle?' he asked.

'You have married all but one of them off, William, playing politics, for all the good it has done you,' Isabelle said, a hint of the steel that characterised her indomitable spirit beneath the sadness.

William frowned. 'Ah, yes, I recollect, Young Belle took the hand of your distant kinsman, Guilbert de Clare, Earl of Gloucester, who fell into my hands at Lincoln…and Sybil, who was named for my mother…what happened to Sybil, Belle?'

'You sought to placate Ranulph of Chester by marrying her to one of Earl Ferrars's lads.'

'Ahh yes.' William stirred awkwardly. 'He that is Ranulph's kin… Chester proved an ingrate, God damn his soul.'

'Tush, William, you should not speak so. Tell me, are you in pain?' Isabelle's tone was concerned. Thus far William had concealed his distemper from her.

'No, my love. 'Tis but grey geese that fly over my grave…'

***

In January 1219 William and Isabelle rode to Westminster. During the journey Isabelle became aware that her husband was seriously ill. He had great difficulty easing himself, he ate little and lost weight. By now his household all knew of the master's diseased state.

'What ails my Lord?' a tearful Thomas had enquired of John D'Earley. That worthy, convinced that William's illness was not only fatal, but owed everything to the betrayal of his former friends, Ranulph of Chester and Peter des Roches, replied with a bitter and brutal frankness, which shocked poor Thomas.

''Tis either or both the galloping knob-rot, or the creeping arse-ache, but whatever I fear it marks the end of my Lord's life.'

Taking up affairs of state, William was obliged to retire to his bed at Candlemas. The doctors Isabelle called in could prescribe nothing but nostrums and while they waggled their heads it was clear that, whether or not they knew the deep-seated source of William's malady, they could do nothing.

To be close to the King William left his bed, painfully mounted a horse and with Isabelle and a modest household, rode east to quarter himself in The Tower. Here he remained until Lent, attended by the faithful Thomas and the closest of his knights. He discussed his Last Will and Testament and made confession weekly, chiefly to Aimery St Maur.

In March he decided to leave London for a quieter place. 'I bethought myself of Caversham, Belle. 'Tis neither Striguil nor Leinster, but it is lovely in the spring.'

And so they came to Caversham by boat, William in one, Isabelle in a second, with the household partly afloat and partly following, a dolorous train of roncins and gloomy servants and sumpters.

Hard behind came King Henry and his Court, to lodge in Reading Abbey, close to Caversham Manor from where, in his sick-bed, William ran the King's government. In close and constant attendance were John D'Earley, John Marshal and Will Marshal. In his last days his other sons arrived, summoned by Isabelle who now slept in William's chamber.

On Easter Monday, William, with Henry at his side, held a Royal Council. Its attendees included Hubert de Burgh, Peter des Roches, Aimery St Maur and the new Legate, the returned Cardinal Pandolpho. Aware than the end was close, William rendered an account of his doings since the death of John and in the service of the young King. Before he expired, he told them, the matter of a Guardian must be settled, for the King had many years yet before attaining his majority.

'My Liege,' interrupted Des Roches, 'your person was placed in my hands…'

'That is not true,' said William, raising himself from his pillows, his face wearing a ghastly expression that stopped Des Roches' mouth. 'You it was, with my Lord of Chester, who begged such a cup to be taken from you that I might drink from it. I and I alone can decide who best to entrust our beloved Henry to…' And here William twisted to smile at the King.

'My Lord…' the boy managed, his eyes full of tears.

'With your permission, Your Grace, I pray you all withdraw, for I am tired and I shall give you my answer and opinion on the morrow.'

Henry rose. 'My Lords and Gentlemen, let us give the Marshal that time to reflect that he requires, and God grant him wisdom in the choice, for I would as fain listen to him than any other man alive.'

The company crossed themselves as the King left the chamber.

It was next morning before William felt able to discuss the question with his family and closest adherents. It was a Sunday and the bells of Reading Abbey could be heard faintly across the water-meadows of the Thames. Shafts of sunlight lit the room and the cool air of spring wafted the scent of new growth into the chamber.

'It is still a chancellery,' William jested, 'and not yet the ante-chamber to the tomb.'

'Have you come to any conclusions, my Lord?' John Marshal asked, his voice full of supressed anxiety. 'The Papal Legate is without and is eager to press you...'

'And he brings word that the King comes hither.'

'Very well. I shall not detain the Legate long. I have given the matter much thought and can see but one answer, given the squabbling and quarrelling nature of most of my Peers, men who ought to know better, having lived the greater parts of their lives through the troubled times of these past years. Perhaps they have not yet lived long enough; perhaps they lack the wit to discern truths hidden to minds clouded by over-learning, letters and their own ambition.'

William opened his eyes and stared at about him. 'My friends, if the land may not be defended by those supposed to defend it, whose false desires lead them in other paths, then it must be defended by the Apostolic See. Had my Lord of Chester proved a more constant friend I should have commended him to you, but his dog was in the manger and he has taken the cross out of envy of me. God's work is mysterious, but it is clearly not His will that Ranulph should take up my mantle.

'Nor is it fitting that I should hand so great a responsibility over to my heir; such a presumption would sit ill with many,' he went on, looking at Will and speaking in a conciliating tone of voice, 'such that I fear for my son's life.' William paused, allowing his words to sink-in.

Placing the Kingdom under Rome secured it from invasion and immeasurably strengthened Henry's position during his minority. Periodically the Kings of the House of Anjou had, for reasons of expedience, done the same thing, but William's entirely voluntary renunciation of power in favour of the church, was done in his lifetime, before he received Holy Unction and while he possessed his wits and his influence. It was his last great act.

Having outlined his intentions, there came a knock upon the chamber door and Will, having ascertained that the King was then arriving, allowed William to ask one last question. 'Do any of you dissent from this my determination?'

They shook their heads and Isabelle, sitting quiet beside him, squeezed his hand as it lay upon the coverlet.

William nodded. 'Admit them,' he commanded.

'Peter des Roches is in their company, Father.'

'He would be,' remarked William, shaking his head. 'Admit them all,' he added.

'Are you sure, Father?' asked Will.

'Aye; I am sure.'

When Henry, Pandolpho and Des Roches had entered, William closed his eyes and began to speak.

After repeating the gist of the argument he had laid before his close following and affinity, he addressed Henry.

'My Lord King, I am shortly to bow my knee before one greater even than thou, so indulge me if I should speak like a father. I abjure you to grow up in Christ, to be worthy of your Crown and Throne, and look to God in Christ and the Holy Ghost to cut short your life should you become like some felonious ancestors that are, alas, in your bloodline.'

William held out his right hand to the King, who took it meekly, murmuring 'Amen to that my Lord Marshal.'

William continued, his voice strong, over-riding the waves of pain made manifest by the sweat pouring down his face.

'I can truly say that I have served you loyally and to the uttermost of my power. I would fain serve you yet if it pleased God to enable me but, as you and all present can see, it is no longer His Will that I should abide longer in this world and I must now make my composition and preparation for redemption according to the teachings of our Holy Mother, the Church.

'It is fitting that I lay down my charge certain that in my successor is one that pleases both God and men, one that is agreeable to our still-divided Baronage…'

William beckoned Pandolpho to approach.

'Therefore, fair sweet Prince, I beg that you place your Kingdom in the hands of God's Vicar here on earth and I have every hope of its prosperity…'

William held out his left hand towards Pandolpho.

'My Lord Cardinal,' William began, only to be interrupted by Des Roches, pushing himself forward to the bedside.

'My Lord Cardinal this is not fitting!' the Bishop protested.

A rustle of indignation moved everyone in the room. Isabelle, who had risen to make way for the King, put a hand out, John Marshal reached for his sword only to realise he was not wearing it, but Will Marshal had his dagger in his hand. Unfazed, Des Roches' arrogance brooked no intimidation as he made his argument.

'If my Lord Marshal is handing over his authority to Holy Church it should first come to me in the absence of the Archbishop of Canterbury, I am besides appointed tutor to the King and it is I who should…'

William roused. 'Stand clear, you dog!' snarled William from his pillow. He was breathing heavily now, exhausted by the effort of coherent thought and its enunciation, but roused to a furious indignation at Des Roches' presumption. 'You of all people do not stand betwixt the King's grace and the Holy Legate! In my renunciation, I hand my office directly to the Apostolic See. My Lord Cardinal, thank God for your presence here; I beseech thee, take the King's hand and lead him in Holy ways for the glory of God and the good of the Kingdom.'

Appalled by Des Roches' intervention and moved by William's words, a stunned silence fell upon the chamber, broken by Pandolpho, who – embarrassed by the Bishop's behaviour - muttered an acceptance of William's decision, called it wise and uttered a benediction at which the entire company crossed themselves, but he got no further, for it was the King who ended the affair.

'My Lord Marshal,' said Henry in a trembling and emotional falsetto. 'We have reposed our trust in you and thank you for your loyalty. As your counsel has ever been, you speak wisely.' Henry turned to Pandolpho, 'My Lord Legate, I willingly submit my Kingdom to the protection and love of the Apostolic See until I come of age. God grant the Holy Father's counsel be as loving as my Lord Marshal's…'

The boy could manage no more, but as they left the chamber, they saw that William was smiling through his pain.

***

268

In the hours that followed, utter silence hung in William's bed-chamber as he lay breathing slowly. Either Isabelle or one of his daughters, all of whom had been summoned to Caversham, sat quietly at his bed-side. The sun set without him taking any sustenance and the hours of darkness fell upon him. Outside his chamber opinion among his following was that he would die in the dawn, but he did not. Before the twilight of the May morning lifted the gloom of the room William stirred. 'Summon the family,' he murmured, 'and John D'Earley.'

His voice was weaker than it had been, but his mind was lucid and his thoughts ordered. He spoke of love, love for Isabelle whom he named as his 'beautiful friend,' love for his sons and daughters, 'for whom he had provided right well,' though there was some difference of opinion over this.

After Isabelle's death, Will would inherit all her lands: the Earldom of Pembroke, Leinster and Striguil; their second son, Richard, was gifted the scattered estates that lay both in England and Normandy granted by the Lionheart; Walter had Goodrich Castle and Gilbert was in Holy Orders. Only young Anselm seemed left out, his father arguing that he might make his way in the world as he, William, had had to do.

Yet to be knighted, Anselm seemed upset and John D'Earley stepped forward. 'My Lord, if I might presume on your son Anselm's behalf. Do you assign him to my mesnie, I shall see him dubbed in due course. If I may presume further, but some allowance to cover the cost of horse-shoes...' D'Earley broke off, his face smiling sadly.

There was a shocked silence among William's family at D'Earley's effrontery. It was too soon after Des Roches' grossly miscalculated intervention for D'Earley's words to sit easily with anyone. But William recognised the brave jest, smiled and lifted a hand, making a gesture towards D'Earley.

'Ever thoughtful John,' he said, turning to Anselm. 'You heard what your good friend John D'Earley asks for in your name; you shall have one hundred and forty pounds a year, enough to maintain you until you make a marriage proper to your standing.' William paused again, looking about him at the ring of pale faces surrounding the bed. The sound of weeping came through the tinnitus that had rung in his ears ever since he had had his casque all but beaten into his skull during his tourneying days.

'And there is yet the maid Joan...' William beckoned his youngest and only unmarried daughter towards his bed-side. 'Wipe away your tears, my chick, I go but on a journey better than a crusade, for my earthly body is shattered and we must make some provision for my little one, eh?' He paused, mastering his own emotions as Isabelle, sitting beside him, wept as uncontrollably as Joan. 'Until Will shall find a husband worthy of you, you shall have land worth thirty pounds a year and two hundred marks to keep you...' William paused. 'There are other bequests besides, Thomas knows of them and they are to those among my mesnie, the most loyal of whom has been John D'Earley... Come hither John, for I have a commission for you.'

D'Earley fell on his knees, took William's extended hand and, weeping, kissed it.

'You shall take horse within the hour. Ride like the wind to Goodrich and leave orders to be sent west to all my castles that it is my last instruction to my castellans that they hold the Southern March in the King's name and check any insolence that may be shown by the Welsh Princes when they learn of my death. Go then to Chepstow; take with you a key which my Lady Isabelle will give you. In our chamber at Chepstow there is a locked chest. It contains cloth with which I would have my body draped at my funeral. Bring it hither and hasten back. Go now!'

John D'Earley rose and, wracked by sobs, stumbled out of the chamber.

William closed his eyes and, once again, he was left to his women. The hours passed and night came on. After dark William called for food and drink. He partook of a little watered wine, and a dish of mushrooms and dried bread, the only thing he could hold down.

Isabelle was sitting with him at dawn, when he rallied and called for more pillows. She summoned help from the ante-chamber. Will and John Marshal, who had been dozing fitfully, rolled in their cloaks like soldiers on campaign, rushed in, thinking the hour had come.

'Pray help my Lord,' Isabelle pleaded, 'he wishes to sit up.'

They got William into a sitting position, aware that despite his malady and the waste to which it had laid his body, he remained a powerful man. It was some moments before he spoke.

'Pray send to Aimery St Maur and request that in all humility I ask his presence here, not being able to come to him.'

'What means this?' asked John Marshal of young Will, his voice low. The younger Marshal looked at his mother, over whose face an expression of pained sadness had swept; it was a profound contrast to the expression of stoic acceptance of God's will that had borne-up her spirit during the preceding days.

Will shrugged. 'I do not know, but I think my mother does...'

As they withdrew again, they heard William ask that Isabelle woke all his daughters and brought them to him. When they had assembled and sat about his bed, he spoke to them individually until Will re-entered the chamber with the news that Aimery St Maur had arrived, whereupon William turned to Isabelle.

'Go, Belle, get it for me now...'

Isabelle's appearance in the ante-chamber again raised the alarm that William's last moments had come, but with a pale, composed face, she swept past them, returning some moments later with a bundle wrapped in linen.

As the door closed behind her John Marshal once again asked what was going on and, once again, Will shrugged his ignorance, at which point Aimery St Maur entered the ante-chamber and they made their respective salutations. St Maur wore a large crucifix about his neck, the cloak of his Order and was girded with his sword. Another came with him, bearing a small, golden box and a Holy Bible.

'Pray tell him that I am come,' said St Maur and Will did as he was bid. William nodded and asking that St Maur be admitted. Will and John Marshal followed the Grand Master of the English Chapter of the Order of Knights Templar into William's presence as he spoke his last words to his wife who was again kneeling at his bed-side.

'Fair Lady, kiss me now, for our lips may never touch again in this world.'

Isabelle bent forward in floods of tears, her reserve broken. As they enjoyed their final moment of intimacy William was sobbing and as Isabelle lifted her face, William touched her cheek one last time. 'Belle, Belle, my beautiful friend,' he murmured. Then raising his voice he said, 'God bless you and all my chickens...' he gestured at his girls and made the sign of the cross above them as they fell to their knees, genuflecting themselves.

'Now go, my sweet, for you know what must be done and that I must now forswear the company of women...'

Unable to speak, Isabelle nodded and rose, shepherding their uncomprehending daughters before her as she left the room. As the women departed, Will came forward.

'Father?'

'Bring forward my Lord Aimery and then assist me into these robes...' William whispered. Beside the bed, where Isabelle had lately sat, the linen bundle lay open. Both Will and John Marshal knew immediately what it was and, coupled with William's dismissal of Isabelle and their daughters, guessed what the Marshal had arranged in total secret.

When they had wrapped William in the white cloak with the red cross of the risen Christ upon its shoulder, Aimery St Maur ordered them to withdraw.

What transpired next was known only to William, St Maur, his assistant, and God the Father, the Son and the Holy Spirit as Aimery inducted the dying man into the Order of Knights Templar.

Afterwards William's heirs were informed of the fact by Aimery and when Will asked his father where he wished to be laid to rest, William indicated Aimery St Maur.

'It is your father's wish that he lies in the Church of the Temple in London, for he is both Knight and Monk now, and will die thus when his time comes.'

William's time came some few hours later, around noon on that Tuesday, 14th May. He died, shriven of his sins, his head in Will's hands, surrounded by his attending knights and Aimery St Maur, Isabelle and their daughters waiting in the ante-chamber. The casement windows were already open to allow his great soul to escape the trammels of this earthly life and fly upwards to heaven.

***

John D'Earley rode into Caversham the following evening having ruined three horses in his headlong ride. He was mortified not to have attended his old master in his last hours, but had the consolation of knowing he had been the last knight to carry out William's ultimate order.

He had brought with him ten ells of silk cloth that, many years earlier, William had brought back from the Holy Land, after travelling thither at the behest of the dying Henry, the so-called Young King, who had never ruled but had spent his entire life in his father's unhappy shadow. When the bundle was unrolled the silk was faded until, some turns into it, the dark lustre of its sheen revealed itself, unaffected by time and storage.

It proved a magnificent covering of William's body as it was taken first to Reading Abbey, to lie in a side chapel. Here Henry's waiting Court did it due reverence at a High Mass before it was placed on a wagon and taken to Westminster by way of Staines at the head of a cavalcade with the banners of William's large mesnie and affinity following. Immediately behind the wagon rode Thomas and Edgar, confidential clerk and secret courier; Isabelle, her ladies and daughters, followed with their own escort. Ahead of the wagon upon which lay William's mortal remains with the dark naevus upon its right shoulder blade, rode John D'Earley, one of William's executors and his most loyal and trusted knight. He bore William's green and gold standard with its red lion rampant, which lifted languidly in the spring breeze.

Mass was sung again at Staines and at Westminster, in St Peter's great abbey-church, and, on 20 May 1219, the second anniversary of the Battle of Lincoln, William's body was escorted to the Temple Church on the Thames's Strand in London. Here had gathered most of the chivalry of England under the Royal Standard of King Henry III. The rites, obsequies and eulogy were led by Stephen Langton, William's old friend, newly returned from Rome and reinstalled as Archbishop of Canterbury.

Above the tomb opened in the chancel, as grown men who had fought each other wept openly, and the King blubbered like the frightened boy he was, Langton pronounced the interment, raising his voice to declare that: 'Here lies the greatest knight of all the world that has lived in our time'.

AFTERWORD

Among William's many bequests, he left land and revenue to the Templars. He had, it may be recalled, founded an Augustinian Priory at Cartmel around 1189 and the Cistercian houses of Duiske and Tintern Parva in Leinster early in the 1200s. He had established a lighthouse at Hook Head in Ireland that ships may have safe passage from Milford Haven to Waterford. But at his death William, despite his piety and his submissions to Holy Church, still technically lay under the excommunication of Bishop Ailbe Ómáelmuaid of Ferns, whose enmity he had incurred years earlier in Leinster. King Henry brought the Bishop to the Temple Church to lift the sentence, but Ailbe refused, causing a public outcry.

William's enemies afterwards pointed to the further manifestation of God's displeasure when, by 1245, the Marshal's line was extinct, but much was owed to another Bishop, that friend turned enemy, Peter des Roches of Winchester, who was implicated in the death of William's second son, Richard.

The Lady Isabelle survived her husband less than a year, dying in February 1220. She lies buried in Tintern Abbey, Gwent, above the lovely River Wye, not far from Chepstow/Striguil.

As for the boy-King, Henry III, his reign seemed set fair under the administration of Peter Des Roches and Hubert de Burgh, but the two quarrelled and De Burgh ousted Des Roches, who went on crusade. In 1232 he returned to England and turned the tables on De Burgh, wresting the government from him. Ever headstrong, Des Roches foolishly applied arbitrary powers reminiscent of King John and fell from power two short years later.

De Burgh's early administration seemed to follow many of William's principles, but the continuing presence of troublesome *routiers*, most notably Falkes de Bréauté, who continued to regard his tenure of castles placed in his hands by William as fiefdoms of his own, plus the growing opportunism of Peter des Roches, caused him immense problems, leading to his procuring Des Roches' dismissal from the King. However, the return of that troublesome priest from Outremer in 1232 and his persuading Henry to exchange De Burgh for himself, led to the eclipse of his political career. Nevertheless, De Burgh had by this time married - as his third wife - the sister of King Alexander of Scotland and had been made Earl of Kent. He died in 1243, four years after his former colleague and later enemy, Des Roches.

Although Henry declared himself of age in 1227, it was not until after his marriage to Eleanor of Provence in 1236 that he took control of his government. Thereafter he failed to heed William's advice and became his father's son, vacillating and too embedded in the House of Anjou's preoccupations with their hereditary lands and overseas adventures. This worked against him and, yet again, fomented opposition from the English Barony who were increasingly conscious of their difference from their Anglo-Norman forbears, imbibing a palpable sense of being English. The upshot of all this was another Baronial revolt, Henry being effectively deprived of his throne after the Battle of Lewes, by Simon de Montfort in 1264.

However, he was rescued from this ignominy the next year when his son Edward (afterwards Edward I, much, much later denominated 'the Hammer of the Scots'), defeated De Montfort and ended the Barons' War on the field of Evesham in August 1265.

Henry, though nominally King again, concentrated his efforts on rebuilding Westminster Abbey. He died in 1272.

Made in the USA
Las Vegas, NV
07 October 2022

56692190R00163